SO JUST BECAUSE YOU HANG AND DO NOTHING ALL DAY DOESN'T MEAN YOU CAN'T FOCUS ON SELF-IMPROVEMENT

- Do a daily job search in five minutes or less.

- Learn how to not start a business with no mon-ay and no ideas.

- Discover different techniques to avoid urgent matters by screwing around.

- Explore the art of the "powerthru" when you want to get through that row of cook-ays.

- Improve your culinary skills by, like, throwing alot of different stuff together and adding stuff on top of that.

- Develop your addiction to coff-ay by leaps and bounds.

THE ODD TODD HANDBOOK.
IT CAN SAVE YOUR LIFE.

the
Odd Todd HANDBOOK

HARD TIMES, SOFT COUCH.

WRITTEN AND ILLUSTRATED
by
Odd Todd

WARNER BOOKS

An AOL Time Warner Company

Copyright © 2003 by Todd Rosenberg

Warner Books, Inc., 1271 Avenue of the Americas, New York, NY 10020

Visit our Web site at www.twbookmark.com.

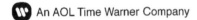 An AOL Time Warner Company

Printed in the United States of America

First Printing: May 2003
10 9 8 7 6 5 4 3

ISBN: 0-446-69079-1
LCCN: 2003101881

Book design by HRoberts Design

dedicated to all

job seekers

everywhere

Acknowledgments

So like I put together this really long list of acknowledgments because it's the only way I know how to do this. All these people helped me alot in doing what I done did in one way or another somewhere along the way . . . so . . .

Special thanks to:

My most excellent editor, John Aherne, and his editorial accomplice, Megan Rickman, who helped me every step of the way and had the most dead-on suggestions and they didn't yell at me alot and they were smart about stuff and they kept me from freaking out too badly and told me when stuff was or wasn't funny and for dealing with my lateness and for buying this friggin book in the first place (and for letting me spell "alot" "alot" even though they're not supposed to).

Rob Golenberg and Bruce Gellman, who are working behind the scenes to try and get blue robe guy on a TV near you. I guess I don't really have to say a TV near you . . . that's more like for movies or whatever. They're both great people and great advisers.

Claire Israel, who has been a great friend and coolio source of frickin funny ideas. And for straightening me out when crazy stopped by to visit.

Stacey Kamen, who not only keeps my site from falling apart but has great insight when I need to "fix" my cartoons. For being a good friend and being honest with me to no fault. And for her laugh.

Mara Leventhal for her patience and understanding and affection and support and sparkle. Without her this book would have come out like three months late.

Woody and Jamie Messinger, who were a great help in shaping the first cartoon with their most excellent ideas, tweaks, and suggestions. Even though my "close friend" Woody tells me all my other cartoons suck—it helps keep me from getting lazy.

Alan Nevins, my book agent, who believed in this book and sold this thing, which kept me from moving home with my parents. He was a huge help in shaping the proposal into something coherent and something publishers actually wanted to buy.

Jeffrey and Keli Papen, who run Peak Webhosting. Without them oddtodd.com would have ceased to exist a long time ago. Switch your site to Peak today. The site is a labor of love for them.

Howard Roberts, who patiently taught me how to prepare print-ready images and used his great creative instincts to put this book together. He done made this book look as excellent as it done do.

My dad, who has always supported everything I do and been there for me with the most excellent advice, and my mom, who called me an artist long before anyone else did . . .

My brother, Dan, and his wife, Jodi, for their enthusiasm and support and friendship and their kids, Brandon and Jordan, who provide maybe the most inspiration of all.

AND totally thanks to all these people for what they did in their own way:

Beau Ambur, Noam Bramson, Vince Calandra, Mike Cohen, Dave Colella, Lauren Corrao, Anne Curry, Judge Beverly Diego, Leslie Eaton, Danny Elfman, Elf Up, Ed Erenberg, Chris Faillace, Adam Flick, Gene Gene, God, Andy Goetz, Goob, Eileen Greene, Kathleen Hackett, Jason Hills, Robyn Hitchcock, Seth Hochman, Chris Irving, Ian Joyner, Myrna June, Frost Keaton, Stephen King, Brian Knapp, Will Kopelman, Janet Komblum, Jeff Lederer, Elliott Lewitt, John Marcom, Mike Markoff, Jainee McCarroll, Peter McHugh, Mep, Jill Merrill, George Michael, Courtney Mota, Vince Neil, Megan Newman, Geoffrey Noles, Mary Kate O'Connell,

Senator Fancy Pants, Lisa Parker, Robin Ophelia Quivers, Jamie Raab, Glenn and Jodie Rappaport, Rage, John Rosano, Rochelle Ross, David Lee Roth, Eric Rubinstein, Penina Sacks, Kyle Scott, Lisa Sorensen, Spongebob, Howard Stern, Abby Terkuhle, Jen Van Vleck, Dave Vernick, Neal Weinberg, Liz Wands, Jeff Wolfman, Shauna Yule, Margy Yuspa, and Rob Zombie.

Also coolio thanks lots to:

Everyone in Laid-Off Land and the TV Message Board including: rosaliecoleman, laughing penguin, poorhouse_bound, briandickens, robotrobinson, irishgirlnyc, colacha, righteousdallaschick, hellbomb kapow, lauren3g, marsala1, marney, DJ, squidboy, Dr. Rocks, staplenut, Pee Jay, calicogirl, melliemel, seebert2002, piperforhire, and evilmachines.

Also mongo thanks to:

Everyone at Warner Books who put up with my lateness, disorganization, scattershot delivery process, and anything else that might have caused your frustration. And thank you to the whole sales department at Warner Books. Thank you and thank you.

I'm really sorry if I left anyone out. I know how it feels cause I'm usually left out of stuff like this. I had to do this really quick cause it was late like everything else. But my apologies really . . .

Introduction

Hi! I'm writing a book! I'm starting it . . . now. Here I go. You ready? Here it is. Ok *go!*

So what's this book about? Well it's about lots of things. It's about doing stuff and not doing stuff. Doing stuff in the morning then doing stuff later in the day. Like in the afternoon and stuff. Then things to do at night . . . and stuff.

Who the hell needs this book? Here's a list. See if you're on it:

- You've been laid off.
- You've just graduated college or grad school and found out that it doesn't really mean alot.
- You're just goofing off and screwing around.
- You're starting a business but not sure what the business is yet.
- You're broke . . . and bored.
- You're considering career options.
- You want to buy a cheap gift for people who sit on their asses all day.
- You have a job and work from a home office (aka screw around most of the day).
- You're retired either voluntarily or involuntarily.
- You think you might get laid off soon and want to be responsible by being prepared.
- You call out sick alot even though you're not sick.
- You like books with pictures.
- You like books with words.
- You like books both with words and pictures.

Here's the thing though. If you're broke and you have your days free, sometimes it's hard to think of what to do on a Tuesday afternoon when you have nothing to do and nowhere to go. Well this book will help you. It's a lifestyle-type-guide sort of thing.

The first thing you need to do with this book is put off reading it till tomorrow morning. Because the book starts in the morning and goes through late night it's best to start reading it tomorrow when you wake up. Use it as a guide for tomorrow. So clear out your nonexistent schedule and go lie down on the couch. Start on the next page tomorrow. Close the book. We're done here for today.

I see you don't know how to follow friggin directions. That's ok. Although I give alot of directions in this book you don't necessarily have to follow them at all. You can just say you did. Or don't even do that. That's one thing cool about this book. You don't have to actually do anything. That's actually kinda the whole point.

But this book will teach you how to have a full day doing stuff and getting practically next to nothing accomplished all from the privacy of your own couch. *But if I don't leave the couch or barely leave the apartment what is there to do?* you ask. Well stop interrupting with your questions. Just read on.

Wait a second, Todd! If you got this fancy-schmancy book contract how is it that you're broke, unemployed guy? Aren't you a like millionaire now? you ask. Didn't I just tell you to stop interrupting? But no, I'm not a millionaire. I'm not even a respectable multi-thousandaire. See when people know you're broke they know they don't have to pay you alot. It's only when you're rich that they pay you alot. See how that works? That's how the world works. And that pretty much sucks. But if you buy this book I can make some mon-ay maybe and write more books and stuff. And if you bought it you should be so psyched cause this book is going to be the best book ever written in the history of all literature. I haven't even written it yet and I know this for a fact! It's going to have pictures! And recipes and all sorts of stuff! The publisher guy told me it needs to be seventy-five thousand words. That should be no prob-lemo. Hold on a sec. How many words is this so far? Lemme check . . . one sec . . . Dags! That's alot of frickin words.

Well I got a ways to go. But you have the time I guess, right?

And thanks for buying this book. Hope you dig it and stuff.

tOdd

THE
Odd Todd HANDBOOK

You're Awake!

Hi! Good morning to you. Hopefully you were able to sleep late. Getting twelve hours of sleep is like totally important to complete a day of doing nothing. Getting twelve hours of sleep is half the battle. But you might have noticed it's before 10:00 A.M. or something. Do not panic. You can go back to sleep. Just relax. Here are a few techniques for getting back to sleepyland:

Switch Pillows

Here's what you need to do. If you're normal you have more than one pillow on your bed. The best thing for you to do to return to sleepyland is switch pillows. If you don't have more than one pillow then you're most

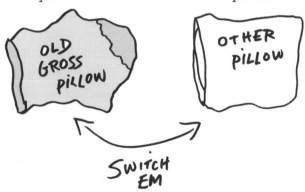

likely in jail or something and they'll probably clang on the bars till you get up anyway so this doesn't apply. (Oh and by the way, if you are an inmate who somehow just got upset by what I just wrote please don't come after me. I didn't mean to tease you about being in jail. I know it sucks enough to be in jail without some stupid jerk with a book teasing you about how you have only one pillow.)

Anyway back to the pillow switching. You most likely have a favorite pillow. I've had mine forever. The feathers aren't like feathers anymore. They're feathermush. I like that. I have to put two pillowcases on it cause it's like yellow and gross with cooties. You probably have a favorite pillow too. What you need to do is swap it for a different pillow. One you like less. This way it's sort of like a new experience for your head. Switching pillows involves using energy and adjusting to a new situation. This should make you sleepy. Go ahead and try it. Put the book down.

Didn't work? Ok here's something else you can do:

Change Directions

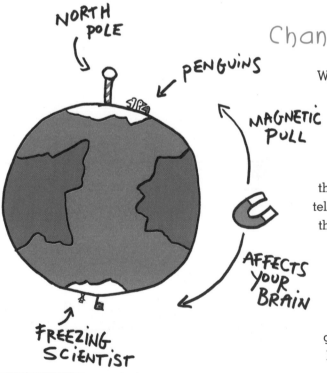

NORTH POLE

PENGUINS

MAGNETIC PULL

AFFECTS YOUR BRAIN

FREEZING SCIENTIST

MY POLARITY THEORY DIAGRAM

When you have alot of free time you begin to like concoct theories about stuff. I have alot of theories now. I have theories about clouds and rain. And I have theories about certain friggin television stations. And I have theories about trees and bugs. But I also have a theory about polarity. I think in the same way we're affected by the tides and the moon we also have something going on with the poles (both North and South) and I think it has something to do with magnets. I sort of half-watched a show about it. So if you completely change directions in bed this will adjust the way your brain responds to the magnetic pull. And this makes you sleepy cause your body uses energy to adjust. And this makes you tired again and stuff. That's my theory anyway. Go try that.

That didn't work either?? Ok. Here's one more technique.

Blankee Adjustment

Your blankee can play a role in helping you fall back to sleep too. The trick to this is taking your blankee flat in your palm and putting it like between your palm and your cheek. Not sure why this works but I took a survey and 84 percent of men and 96 percent of women fall back to sleep immediately if they do this. Ok I didn't really take a poll but if I did I'm pretty sure those numbers are accurate give or take 80 percent. Blankee to cheek and you're off to dreamland. Try that . . .

That didn't work either?? Wow. Ok. Here's the last resort.

Think of Stuff

Sometimes it helps you fall back to sleep if you just try and think of stuff. It's almost like trying to get dreams started while you're still awake. Think about being a superhero (Batman, Wonder Woman, or Gleek) or think about other stuff like: Imagine you're mini-sized inside a dollhouse sitting in a little chair watching a little TV that has a TV show starring you sitting in a dollhouse in a chair watching a little TV. Or maybe think about like you're on the moon sitting in a lawn chair in a crater with a cooler filled with grenades and you're lobbing them around all willy-nilly weightlessly. Eventually this line of thinking will help you grab a dream out of the dream vault and it will make you sleepy. Go ahead put the book down and think of stuff. See if that works.

Nope, huh? Maybe you had a really intense dream and stuff and that's why you can't get back to sleep. Luckily I'm an expert in like interpreting dreams so here's a guide to that.

Dream Interpretations

Here are interpretations of three very common dreams. You most likely just had one of these three dreams:

THAT DREAM SHOULD LOOK LIKE THIS

DREAM #1:

You dreamed that you were on a mountaintop and the sky was fire red and there were giant bizarre birds flying around and there was some mysterious person to your right who looked very familiar (maybe from high school or something) but you can't remember who that person is and there is like a podium and a small crowd gathered and the audience seems to be all lizards or dragons (anything reptilian *except snakes*) and the person giving the speech is the "Clam King."

Interpretation: This very common dream means good fortune is coming your way. You can expect to receive a check for a large amount of money or perhaps find something valuable in the street like one of those really old coins that crazy people will pay a ton of money for. Be on the lookout. I suggest you walk around looking at the ground.

DREAM #2:

You dreamed that you were swimming in a river trying to cross the river but the current was really strong and you noticed you have all these scales on you like fish scales and then you noticed you have gills and you can breathe underwater and when you swim down you find this like big tube and you climb in and in that tube there are little tricycles and you ride down the tunnel and when you come out the other side you're in an underwater fish arena and you're a freak clown in the Cirque d'Atlantis.

FREAK CLOWN

CIRQUE D'ATLANTIS

Interpretation: This very common dream means bad news. A dream like this means that you can plan to embarrass yourself *big time* in the next week or so. This could be falling down in the street or while climbing up steps. This could involve spilling on yourself or on others or both. Or perhaps you might say something stupid and wish you never said what you just said, which is what you'll think after you say it.

THAT DREAM SHOULD LOOK SOMETHING LIKE THAT

(EXCEPT THOSE THINGS LOOK MORE LIKE LADYBUGS AND THERE ARE THOUSANDS OF 'EM)

DREAM #3:

You dreamed that it's all dark and the phone rings. You know you don't want to answer the phone but you can't help yourself so you do it anyway. Once you take the phone off the hook the room lights up and you're in a room full of people in like anti-radiation suits or something and you can hear them all breathing. One approaches you with what looks like a magic wand with a gold star on the end and when you look into the star it gets bigger and bigger till it takes over the whole room and the whole room is gold and it's filled with ladybugs.

Interpretation: Many people have asked me about this common dream and it has two different kinds of interpretation. If you're a guy it means that you're a big liar and you're going to get caught because your web of lies is unraveling. Try and keep them straight in your head or you're going to trip up and get nabbed. If you're a girl this dream means that you have a secret admirer.

If you did not have one of the above dreams but you did dream about people, or plants, things, or situations in general, this means either good luck is coming your way or you shouldn't leave the house till next Tuesday.

17 COMMON DREAM SYMBOLS AND WHAT THEY MEAN

1. Mothra or any insect monsters = Time to clip your toenails.
2. Smushed fruit = You may break out in a rash or hives.
3. Flying while wearing a tutu or any ballet costume = Test your home for radon.
4. Bananas or banana peels = Run from rabbits.
5. Underground gorillas = You need to go out and buy a plant immediately.
6. Striking out at baseball = Treat yourself to a strip club.
7. Boobs = Boobs.
8. Being chased by birds = You are falling in love.
9. Flags or flagpoles = You masturbate one time too many per day.
10. Breaking glass = Go back to the store and return what you stole.
11. Dreaming of being asleep and dreaming = Cut back on daily naps by one.
12. Falling off a cliff = It was a good thing you didn't get that last job.
13. Eating at a buffet = If you rub your belly it will bring you good luck. This only works three times.
14. Disco dancing in 1975 = Brush your tongue once a week.
15. Giant windup toy = If you're temping . . . quit today.
16. Artichokes = You're about to do something great. Go and do it.
17. Pringles and fudge stripe cook-ays = All is well in the world.

DREAM INTERPRETATION CHART

DREAMING OF: · **MEANS:**

MOTHRA OR INSECT MONSTER → TIME TO CLIP TOENAILS

BANANAS → BUNNIES WILL BRING BAD LUCK

BOOBS → BOOBS

PRINGLES POTATO CRISPS + → ALL IS WELL IN THE WORLD

Ok You've Decided to Get Out of Bed!

Take it slow and easy on yourself. You can pull a back muscle or anything can happen right now. Just sit on the edge of your bed for a good five minutes. Relax. Then when you feel ready get on up.

First things first. Put on your robe. If you don't have a robe then go outside and buy one right now. You will not be able to continue with this book without a robe. If you don't have mon-ay for a robe don't worry. Make some calls to your parents or some older relatives. (More on this later.) They always have lots of extra robes. The uglier and rattier the better. That way you don't worry about stains and stuff. *Do not* continue reading this book without a robe. Go get one. I'll wait here . . . and go through your stuff.

The Robe

The robe is the dress code if you're currently doing nothing professionally. It's a perfect outfit for a number of reasons besides the fact that I think they're snazzy. The main reason robes are good is cause they're easy to put on. Many people make the mistake of putting on full outdoor outfits just to hang around the house. Getting dressed is the first mistake you can make during the day. Here is why a robe works so well for this lifestyle:

8

- Going through the hassle of getting dressed is wasted energy. You have a busy day ahead of you doing nothing and you need to save energy. The pulling on of the pants or getting all tangled up in a shirt for twenty minutes is a hassle you don't need right now. Plus if you're like me you can spin around and knock over a lamp just trying to put on a sweatshirt.
- Robes usually have big pockets for stuff. Like you can keep the remote control in one pocket and candy in the other. If you do decide to use a pocket for candy I would recommend something like Skittles or M&Ms. Gummy candy gets all linty so I would avoid that. Mini-windup toys also are great to store in a robe.
- Wearing the robe prevents you from going outside. If you head outside in your robe you run the risk of bumping into someone you know. If you're in your robe this can be an awkward situation as conversation will be difficult. You've already answered the common questions just by your attire. Questions like: "How's things?" "What have you been up to?" "Where are you working now?" "What are you up to today?" Etc.

Ok now that you're in your robe you probably have to pee. Put the book down and go pee. I'll wait here. I don't want to go in the bathroom with you. Actually, who am I fooling? I figure that's where this book is going to live, in most cases.

Now we're ready to get started with the day. You might feel a bit tired even though you just slept like twelve hours. This is normal. It's called *oversleeping* and it is essential to this lifestyle. Luckily there is a cure. It's called coff-ay.

10:45 A.M.
Coff-Ay

Some people like going outside to get coff-ay but I don't think this is a good idea for a number of reasons.

- Outside is unpredictable. Anything can happen to you when you go outside. I read about this one guy who was walking down the street getting coff-ay and a lead pipe fell off a construction site and went halfway through his head. He was totally fine except now he has Tourette's syndrome and has to walk around with a pipe sticking out of his head. That stuff can happen. I don't want to make you paranoid or anything but . . . is it worth the risk? Think about it next time you head out for coff-ay. Need another reason?
- **STAYING INSIDE SAVES YOU MON-AY. THAT'S RULE #1:** If you go outside for coff-ay you can spend mon-ay along the way and a simple outing for a cup of coff-ay can end up costing you like fifty dollars. Here are some things that can get your mon-ay along the way: three-card monte, drugstores, bumping into a friend you owe mon-ay to, losing your wallet or pocketbook altogether, getting pickpocketed, getting a desperate need for a toy race track with loop da loop (if

you're a guy), desperate need to get some My Pretty Pony stuff (if you're a girl). All these distractions can be costly.

- The true coff-ay experience is an all-day-long process. You'll need to drink like two to three pots over the course of the day. You can't buy three pots of coff-ay outside cause it costs too much mon-ay and it would be a hassle to carry. Even if you could the coff-ay would get cold and you'd have to microwave it and microwaved coff-ay causes rashes.

- Sometimes you go into a coff-ay place and things go wrong. Because you don't understand the menu. It's too much all of a sudden. You panic. You try to took normal. Like you understand. You put your hands on the counter and accidentally knock over their tip jar. You go to pick up the quarters and stuff and whomp your head on the counter. You're dazed but still conscious. You stagger backwards and knock into a table, spilling someone's coff-ay all over their notebook. They scream, "My masterpiece!" You turn to apologize and fall backwards smashing through the glass cabinet containing the pastries. You see an opportunity and grab a black-and-white cook-ay and take a big bite. The coff-ay guy grabs you by the shirt and pulls you out of the case. "What the hell is your problem?!" he asks. You struggle and break free shoving people out of the way. Some girl falls into the lap of some guy. He gropes her by accident. She picks up a cup of coff-ay and splashes it in his face. He screams, "My eyes!" You're out the door and running five blocks just to get away (actually not five blocks, more like five steps before you're all winded). You lie down in the street to catch your breath. You're covered in coff-ay stains and gasping for air. You don't know why you left the house. You pass out.

So be aware. You didn't hear it from me. Stay inside.
Make yer own dang coff-ay and play this game . . .

THE GAME OF COFF-AY

START!

YOU FOUND A CLEAN CUP! AHEAD 2

BEANS GRINDED ROLL AGAIN!

NO SUGAR! LOSE A TURN

THE MILK IS SPOILED! BACK 1

BLEH!

FROGS ARE EVERYWHERE! YOU LOSE!

FANCY MOUSE WITH SNORKLE! AHEAD 2

GOTTA PEE LOSE A TURN

IT'S DECAF BACK THREE

SMELLS GOOD! ROLL!

TOO STRONG BACK ONE

FELL ASLEEP LOSE A TURN

KITCHEN ON FIRE! RUN AWAY!

ZZZZZ...

YOU WIN! DRINK UP!

HOW TO PLAY:

ROLL DICE AND PLAY!

(IF YOU DON'T HAVE DICE JUST THINK OF A NUMBER ONE TO SIX IN YOUR HEAD REALLY FAST. IF YOU DO IT FAST ENOUGH THE NUMBER WILL BE A SURPRISE TO YOU... ESPECIALLY IF YOU'RE WIRED ON COFF-AY.)

12

Modern Wallstaring

This morning ritual is like meditation. The key is to focus on a single spot on the wall and block out all other thoughts. Sometimes it's hard to clear your brain out and think about nothing. You might get a thought floating in like, *Oh shit! How will I pay my credit card bills?* What you need to do is push that thought aside and sip coff-ay. You might get a knock on your door from your landlord asking you where the friggin rent is. Just ignore it, stay quiet, and sip coff-ay. Till you find what I like to call the "Coff-ay Zen Zone." It might take you some time to achieve the spiritual center for this. Don't worry. Push that thought aside too. You have plenty of time and plenty of coff-ay.

WALLSTARING GOAL

WALL

INSIDE YOUR HEAD

SO WHAT'S ON THE AGENDA TODAY?

After five or six cups of coff-ay you might feel your brain speeding up. This is why you should limit the amount of coff-ay you drink while wall-staring to like two cups. This way you won't get distracted by your brain struggling to think of stuff cause it's getting all juiced up and psyched up.

A HISTORY OF WALLSTARING

400,000 BC
EARLY MAN HAS NOTHING BETTER TO DO

573
MERLIN'S BROTHER LENNY TRIES ALL DAY TO CAST A SPELL ON THE WALL

777
MRS. HUN STARES AT WALL ALL PISSED AT ATTILA

1846
SLOW COUSIN JED TOLD TO STARE AT WALL WHILE GOATS WERE VIOLATED BY COOTER & EARL

2003-
MODERN MAN HAS NOTHING BETTER TO DO

11:03 A.M.

Morning Activities

Showering

Most people take a shower first thing in the morning. You are not one of those people. The shower needs to be saved till midday. We'll get to that in a bit.

Teeth Brushing

RULE #2: YOU SHOULD ALWAYS BRUSH YOUR TEETH.

If you decide against this for an extended period of time your teeth will fall out and that would suck cause you couldn't eat potato chips with no teeth. You'd have to eat friggin mashed potatoes—which is ok too but it's always good to have choices. Don't get lazy about your teeth!

Here's a way you can save a few bucks. You know on commercials for like Aquafresh or whatever there's this like big S-shaped thing on the toothbrush? Well that's friggin bull! You don't need that much toothpaste! It's all globby globbed. A scam so it looks nice on your toothbrush and they make you use more of it! Revolt!

When I brush my teeth I like to hum songs. Here are a few songs I hum while brushing my teeth:

TEETH BRUSH SONG

I'M SINGING A SONG ABOUT
BRUSHING MY TEETH
BRUSHING MY TEETH
THIS IS MY TEETH BRUSH SONG
(REPEAT)
MAKE THEM WHITE
MAKE THEM BRIGHT
GIVE THEM EXTRA CHOMPY BITE
OH I'M SINGING A SONG ABOUT
BRUSHING MY TEETH
THIS IS... MY TEETH BRUSH...
SONNN..... GUH!

- Prince, "Kiss." It's good to do a quick up-and-down during the guitar strummy part before he goes "Kiss." Yknow that part?
- Duran Duran, "Rio." I like humming this song cause it makes me think of the video with Simon Le Bon on the front of the boat. And it looks all refreshing. Like tooth brushing is.
- Southern Culture on the Skids, "Walk Like a Camel." Because it's fun to strut around like a camel when you're brushing your teeth while humming the song.

Flossing

Everyone says that flossing is good. But I almost never do it. I once knew a guy who sneezed while flossing and he inhaled the floss. He almost died. If he had, he would have been embarrassed. But there's other things you can do with floss:

- You can use it as a leash for your bug.
- You can tie it around a heart made of clay that says LOOK UP then throw it out the window and fish for dates.
- You can poke a hole in a dollar bill and thread it through and tape it down. Then use it in machines that take dollars. Once you get your soda or songs or whatever then yank it back out. Not sure if this works and it is illegal. I didn't tell you to do this.

THREE OTHER USES FOR FLOSS

BUG LEASH

DATE BAIT

DUSTBALL LASSO

Brushing Your Hair

I don't really have alot of hair left but I can give you recommendations from memory. If you're not doing anything today brushing your hair is wasted energy. You might want to rethink this activity. You want to either shave your head or leave your hair wild looking. This way if your landlord bothers you for rent or whatever he might be scared thinking you're crazy. Having other people believe you're crazy is always a plus—especially if you owe them mon-ay and stuff.

If you're a chick, make your hair as wild as possible. Most guys think that is when your hair looks best anyways. That's what's backwards about stuff. Girls will go about "fixing" their hair when it looks cutest all messy.

Doing Nothing

RULE #3: DOING ANYTHING BESIDES DOING NOTHING IN YOUR OWN WAY IS NOT DOING NOTHING. IT'S DOING SOMETHING.

You've already accomplished alot today with the waking up stuff and the pillow switching and all that. I think you might need to relax for a while. I would recommend continuing your day by doing nothing.

But people should know that doing nothing is in fact what you're doing. Sometimes you can get a phone call and the person will ask what you're doing and if you say "doing nothing" this is sometimes misunderstood and people assume that you actually want to do something besides nothing. They don't realize that the something you are doing *is* nothing. I would avoid telling people you're ever "doing nothing." Always have a backup

DANGER

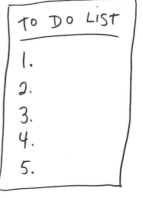

TO DO LIST

1.
2.
3.
4.
5.

UMMM....

plan for when people ask what you're doing so your valuable nothing time isn't all wrecked and stuff.

RULE #4: LYING AND DENYING WILL COME UP ALOT IN THIS LIFESTYLE.

Here are some good excuses:

"I'm taking my cat to the vet." Warning: Only a good lie if you actually have a cat. If you mess up and use this lie by accident and the person says, "You have a cat?" just hang up the phone. When she calls back pretend you weren't on the phone with her just now. If she calls you a liar then call her a liar. Then yell, "One second!" Then say, "Hey I gotta go." But if you have a cat this excuse rocks. Ain't nobody wanna go with you to the vet with your sick throw-up cat.

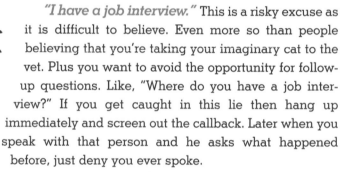

"I have a job interview." This is a risky excuse as it is difficult to believe. Even more so than people believing that you're taking your imaginary cat to the vet. Plus you want to avoid the opportunity for follow-up questions. Like, "Where do you have a job interview?" If you get caught in this lie then hang up immediately and screen out the callback. Later when you speak with that person and he asks what happened before, just deny you ever spoke.

"I'm waiting for the cable guy." This is a good one. Quick. Concise. Important. Believable. People know this is an all-day thing. You can use this excuse a few days in a row and people will still believe it.

But why not just say, "I'm doing nothing," and leave it at that you ask? First off, I told you once to stop interrupting. Don't make me make you return the book. (Don't return the book. Just kidding. I didn't mean to be rude.)

Second, here's why you don't ever say, "I'm doing nothing." In my experience, people assume you're now free to help them. Your day of doing nothing can be ruined by the following statements:

- "Oh good! Can you help me move a couch?" = Day ruined.
- "Oh. I need a favor. Can I come over and use your computer?" = Day ruined.
- "Hey! I gotta take my cat to the vet. Will you come with me?" = Day ruined + 1 throw-up cat.

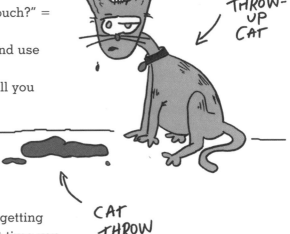

THROW-UP CAT

CAT THROW UP

Or some think this might be an invitation by you to lecture you.

- "Are you seriously doing nothing? I'm getting concerned about you. When is the last time you left the house?" . . . Blah . . . blah . . . blah.

All of this disrupts your time doing nothing and might wreck your whole day. It might make you worry and worrying is not doing nothing. So while you're reading this book I would either screen calls or answer the phone rushed like you just got back or are running out the door. And be prepared with the excuses above.

Doing Nothing on the Couch

Doing nothing is sometimes difficult and it takes practice and preparation. Some people feel they might be incapable of doing nothing. They feel guilt over staying inside all day. If you are one of these people do not worry. You can do nothing. You just have to think positively about it and quiet the voice in your head that is calling you lazy. The trick is to chalk up the little incidental things as major accomplishments.

YOU GO HERE NOW

ENJOY

Unfortunately doing nothing involves some preparation. Most likely, you're going to want to do nothing on the couch. But the trick to lying on the couch is not having to get off the couch till you really have to. So being prepared with supplies to help you do nothing is essential.

DRINKS

You might find lying on the couch makes you thirsty. I would recommend getting yourself water or blue Gatorade. Make sure you bring alot with you to set on your coff-ay table. Most regular glasses are too small so I would bring a few glasses or wash out a spaghetti sauce jar and have that be your water glass. You can substitute the drink of your choice. There is flexibility there. But considering that it is pre-noon I would avoid alcoholic beverages. If you're filling your spaghetti sauce jar with whiskey then this is not a good way to do nothing. This is doing something. It's called *getting drunk.* And it's too early for that.

It's 11:05 AM AND THAT ⟨HIC⟩ LiTTLE ELF AND ME ARE GONNA SPEND SOME QUALITY TIME!

← NOT DOING NOTHING

SNACKS

Although it's not lunchtime yet you'll probably get hungry while sitting on the couch. Here are a few snack treats to have on hand that could also qualify as breakfast or whatever.

Pretzels and Wasabi Peas Combination

I like pretzels and I also like wasabi peas. Wasabi peas might be difficult to find so you've gotta ask around. But they're way good. They're packed in green packaging and have Chinese writing on the bag. I had my Chinese friend interpret the Chinese and it translates to "Wasabi Peas." Take the bowl and dump the peas in the bowl. Then take your pretzels (either twists or nuggets) and dump them in the bowl. Mix it up. It's good.

WASABI PEAS LOOK LIKE THIS

Crunch Berries

Here's the trick to this. First off, you have to have Crunch Berries in your place. If you don't have cereal then skip this recipe. What you do is you bring the box over to the coff-ay table and put it down. Grab handfuls and fill your mouth as much as possible. This avoids too much of the back-and-forth between getting the cereal and eating the cereal. Use your mouth as storage.

If you want to get fancy you can combine the Crunch Berries with milk. I find this is best to do in your mouth. Handful of cereal then sip the milk. This way you are not limited to the "bowl" thing. And you don't need a spoon. And it doesn't produce dirty dishes. You can mix it up in your mouth. It's good.

CAPN CRUNCH'S
CRUNCH BERRIES

Pringles and Fudge Stripe Cook-ays

These two go surprisingly well together. But be warned! You might feel adventurous in the supermarket and try to branch out to the "other flavors" of Pringles. I would avoid this. Go with original. Just bring both the can of Pringles and full package of cook-ays to the couch. Left hand goes Pringles. Right hand goes cook-ays. Left right left right just like in the army. Except you're not in the army. Not even close.

PRINGLES
POTATO CRISPS

WARNING ABOUT SNACK ALTERNATIVES

You might have other food preferences to use for breakfast or whatever. Other types of snacks. This is ok. I find that people sometimes like stuff that other people don't like. That's a fact. As long as your snack comes in a package and doesn't grow on trees you're good to go. If you're not "cooking" or "slicing" anything feel free to choose your own. But if you find yourself cooking or slicing this is not doing nothing. This is cooking and slicing and plates and silverware. Be warned that this sucks. Not only is it an activity to prepare the snacks but it also involves cleaning up, which can interfere with your doing nothing a week from now when you actually decide to do your frickin dishes.

THE ART OF THE POWERTHRU

Sometimes when you're on the couch you might feel like you've eaten too much too fast. Or perhaps you feel full but you still have plenty of cook-ays left. This causes a dilemma. You want to eat more but somehow your body is telling you you've had enough. This is when you have to take control and get motivated and launch what I like to call the powerthru. You have to powerthru that row of cook-ays. You have to powerthru that second half of the can of Pringles. Start off with a deep breath with your eyes closed. Release. Deep breath again. Release. Then just dive right in and start slowly and methodically going powerthru. You can do this. Plus after you finish the box of cook-ays you'll feel a sense of accomplishment, which is always nice to chalk up while doing nothing as it alleviates some of the guilt about . . . doing nothing.

Now that we're set with the supplies, drink, and appropriate cautions there are other things you will need around you for doing nothing.

OTHER OPTIONAL SUPPLIES NEEDED FOR MAXIMIZING YOUR DOING NOTHING EXPERIENCE

I would suggest having these things around you during couch time:

- The phone
- Magazines
- A SuperBall
- Crayons and construction paper
- Sunglasses
- Two pencils (drumsticks)
- A flashlight
- Couch blankee
- World atlas
- Playing cards (nudey chicks)
- Ant farm
- Cowboy hat
- Hockey stick (or broom handle)
- Slinky
- Toy Spider-Man Web Blasters
- Leatherman pocket tool
- Mints
- Sparklers
- Dice
- Two Matchbox cars
- Yellow yarn
- Walkman
- Bug spray
- Super Soaker filled with paint
- Bullwhip
- Red Bull
- A bullfrog
- Paper clips

THINGS TO HAVE AROUND DURING COUCH TIME

PAPER FOR PAPER AIRPLANES

RUBBERBANDS FOR BUG HUNTING

HARMONICA FOR BLUES

KABANGERS FOR COMMERCIAL BREAKS

SPONGE FOR SPONGING

BOBBLE HEAD FOR BOBBLING

FAKE MUSTACHE FOR ANGRY LANDLORD VISITS

After a while of doing nothing you might feel some motivation to actually do something. Take your time till moving on to the next section. You don't want to strain yourself or stress yourself out. Take it easy. Breathe deep. Ok, turn the page. We're going to do something . . .

23

12:09 P.M.

Doing Stuff

The first thing we're going to do is look for a job. The reason why is we just need to get this out of the way. If you have a job already but don't like your job you'll find some nice tips to help you find a new job. If you're totally happy with what you do for a living and are working hard at a job you like and are a morning person or whatever then just return this book. There's nothing to see here. Just move on.

RULE #5: IT IS EXPECTED FOR YOU TO LIE ON YOUR RÉSUMÉ.

Ok. So you need a new job. No problem. First let's fix up your résumé a bit. You know how your résumé has those stupid bullshit bulletpoint things? Below is a word match thing to help you beef up your résumé. Just pick any phrase from each column and make up your own dang sentences. I can't do everything for you.

A	B	C	D	E
Spearheaded	a dynamic	marketing initiative	to better enhance	corporate goals
Initiated	a unique	IT solution	to increase	departmental performance
Developed	a profitable	B2B program	to cultivate	individual goals
Launched	a turnkey	advertising plan	to expand	overall performance
Created	a streamlined	content partnership	to capture	revenue goals
Coordinated	a groundbreaking	new platform	to aggregate	sales goals
Managed	an integrated	promotional product	to achieve	overall profits
Supervised	a highly effective	promotion	to strengthen	the core business

Just jumble up those words in any way you like and bam! You have a brand new résumé. And while you're at it give yourself a promotion too. Were you a Manager? Now you're a Director. Were you an Account Executive? Congrats! You're now a Departmental Manager. Whatever you want! Also you made ten grand more than you thought! Tell em that too!

Might as well be a little dishonest. Worst-case scenario they find out and you won't get the job. Who wants to work for a place that doesn't trust you in the first place?

Ok now that was that. As for where to send your résumé you can go through the traditional channels by sending it around online or responding to ads in the paper. But here are some unique innovative résumé circulation methods:

- Hand them out on the bus with Hershey's Kisses.
- Throw a stack of em up in the air and let Mother Nature network them for you.
- Have someone write your résumé on your back in Magic Marker. If you get an interview and someone asks to see your résumé just rip your shirt off, turn around, and flex hard! It shows you mean business.
- Have your résumé delivered to an HR department disguised as a subpoena. Just send a friend into their office and have her hand the résumé over. She should say, "You've been served." Then walk out. When the HR people see it's just your résumé they'll be so relieved they're not in trouble that they'll hire you right there on the spot!
- On the first side have your résumé, on the back have a pizza menu. Distribute them in corporate parking lots. Have the number of the pizza place be your home phone. When they call for pizza convince them to hire you. If they're not into that try and sell em a pizza or something.

RÉSUMÉ

PIZZA

Here's a job search game for ya.

JOB SEARCH GAME

- PUT ON YOUR COAT— HIRING FREEZE.
- YOUR FRIEND WHO'S SMARTER THAN YOU JUST APPLIED FOR THE SAME JOB
- YOU GOT A LETTER INFORMING YOU THAT YOU DON'T QUALIFY FOR A FORM LETTER REJECTION.
- WEARING AN APRON AT YOUR NEXT JOB IS LIKELY
- YOU GOT THE JOB!
- YOU REALIZE YOU DON'T KNOW WHAT SECTION OF THE WANT ADS TO EVEN LOOK IN
- HR PERSON IS SOMEONE YOU KNEW IN HIGH SCHOOL— YOU HATED EACH OTHER
- YOU FOUND 3 TYPOS AFTER SENDING OFF A BATCH OF RÉSUMÉS
- YOUR KEY CONTACT JUST GOT THE AX.

HOW TO PLAY: STAND OVER BOARD.
DROP A PEANUT ON THE BOARD.
EAT PEANUT.
REPEAT.

Just in case you have an issue with getting a regular job: Here's a listing of alternative careers that always sounded kind of cool to me.

- Lobsterman
- Doctor
- Psychic
- Minor-league baseball player
- Fry cook
- Balloonist
- Archaeologist
- Cruise ship steward
- Peace Corps volunteer
- Freelance writer
- Sculptor
- Porn director
- Porn movie reviewer
- Professional bowler
- King
- Plumber
- Tour guide

After you think of a bunch of reasons why these jobs might be difficult to find, you might start thinking about some other ways to make a living like:

MAD INVENTOR

VIDEO GAME TESTER

PORN STAR

TEMP

BOUNCER

GUY IN CHICKEN SUIT

GOAT HERDER

or . . .

Interviewing Do's and Don'ts

If you do happen to get an interview I have prepared a list of do's and don'ts for the interviewing process.

DO dress nicely and appropriately for that particular office.

DO NOT steal anything.

DO be prepared by doing extensive research on the company.

DO NOT comment on the interviewer's eyes, hair, or breasts.

DO think about your answer before answering questions.

DO NOT answer any question with "Huh?," "Who knows?," or "That's a stupid question. You're stupid."

DO sit up straight but relax.

DO NOT put your feet up on the desk or spin around in your chair and say "Wheee!"

DO find out about the benefits the company may be offering.

DO NOT argue to get more vacation days during the first interview.

DO feel free to talk about the skills you gained from your previous job.

DO NOT talk about how you got yourself fired because your boss was a "stupid ass."

DO smile. It's ok to have a good time during an interview.

DO NOT tell jokes that contain the words *hooters* or *fart.*

DO let the interviewer get to know you on a personal level to a certain degree.

DO NOT let him know what you're really like.

DO follow up with a thank-you letter. Handwritten is still preferred.

DO NOT call every day all psycho giving threatening ultimatums.

DO thank the interviewer before leaving and say you hope to hear from her soon.

DO NOT say anything racist, sexist, or make remarks about how the office seems "sucky."

DO remain positive. Things happen for a reason and if you don't get a job you will find the right one eventually.

DO NOT beat yourself up. Things aren't easy right now. You have talents that will be appreciated.

THE 5-MINUTE INTERVIEW
DISASTERHAIR
DOESN'T LISTEN TO QUESTIONS. TOO DISTRACTED BY DOPEY JERK INTERVIEWER
BAGGY EYES FROM WORRY ABOUT NOT HAVING A JOB
MUSTARD
INAPPROPRIATE DRESS
FIDGETY

Consider a Life of Crime

You might start to think the best thing to do is pursue a life of crime. Criminals seem to live pretty well until they get caught and thrown in the slam. But they get to make their own hours and the work often involves travel. Here are some common reasons not to become a common criminal:

Pimping or Hooking

- WHERE AM MY HOES?
I MEAN...
BE...
WHERE BE
MY HOES?

Being a pimp or a hooker usually isn't a great job. Both jobs will make your mother cry. And fashionwise you're going to one day take a look at your wardrobe and think, "Jeez louise do I have bad taste or what?" Plus, both jobs can get you like arrested.

**RULE # 5½:
ANY JOB THAT CAN
GET YOU ARRESTED IS
SOMETHING TO BE
AVOIDED.**

If you're like a Greenpeace activist or something trying to save the whales or something, then maybe that's something to pimp or hook for. In fact, if you're going to be a pimp or a hooker, do it for Greenpeace. Those people all hang out in the Arctic Circle and probably get lonely alot. But if you don't like fighting don't be a pimp. Most likely at some point someone will smack your head down on the friggin hood of a car or something.

Scam Artist

I read about this scammer dude who wrote up a letter saying that he was in "your restaurant" last week and some waitress spilled on him. He asked to be reimbursed for the dry-cleaning expense. Also enclosed was a Xerox copy of a dry cleaner's receipt for twelve bucks. He sent this out to hundreds of thousands of restaurants and received tons of checks for twelve dollars. Good idea, right? Except he got caught and now is doing hard time. Even the best of scams can get you busted. And your scam wouldn't be as good as that one. Trust me.

SO LIKE... YOU GIVE ME TEN DOLLARS AND THEN I GIVE YOU NINE DOLLARS AND NINE DIMES...

THAT'S YOUR SCAM?

I'M NEW...

SCAMMER

Coke Dealer

Dealing coke seems like an easy way to make a buck too. You might think you're actually providing a service for your community and stuff. You can rationalize this in your head that way. That you're just doing what someone else would be doing. And you get laid and you get to cut the line at clubs and stuff. Except the thing about it is you have a conscience and your conscience will tell you bad things about you all day long. Your conscience will tell you that you're a bad person and stuff for dealing coke. You'll be up all night worrying that the people you dealt coke to don't do too much and stuff. Who needs a headache like that? Plus getting punched in the face or shot at is fairly common when you're a coke dealer. If you're afraid of bullets this probably isn't for you. Plus when you're a coke dealer you have fake friends.

COKE DEALER

I'M POP...POP... POPULAR...

31

OH...ALSO ARE YOU GUYS HIRING?

Bank Robber

Bank robber seems cool! You get psyched up then go barging through the door of a bank and yell, "Nobody move! This is a robbery!" (just like the guy in *Pulp Fiction*). You have some Halloween mask on. Everyone gets down on the floor and you scurry over the countertop with a sack and tell someone to fill the bag. You have rock music playing in your head. You grab the bag full of money and jump off the counter but you trip and fall down and mess up your knee. You get yourself to your feet and limp-run outside but when you get to your get-away car you see that you locked your keys inside. You break the driver's window with the gun butt but some glass shatters outward and a shard gets in your eye. You drop the gun as you put your hand to your head. Your eye stings so bad you get a rumbling in your head that almost drowns out the police sirens. You look down in the car with your one good eye and see shards of glass all over the driver's seat. You can't sit down there so you head out on foot, limping with one hand to your eye and the other holding on to the bag. Cops surround you and tell you to put your hands up but cause you're so disoriented you go to get your wallet out instead. The cops think you're going for your gun and open up on you. As your body gets riddled with bullets you realize you have chosen the wrong career. Big-time.

Start a Billing Service

I always thought it would be a good idea to start a billing service. You make up a bill like this:

INVOICE FOR SERVICES NOT ORDERED NOR DELIVERED. $$

and send it off to major companies. I would think most companies are messed up enough to just pay it. Especially if it's a small amount. The accounting department might think they're the ones that messed up cause they don't know what the hell it is. They might be too embarrassed to admit that they don't know where the hell they're getting bills from.

Good idea right? Wrong. See most companies are in financial ruin right now and your crappy little invoice will just take them down one notch more. Which means they don't hire anyone for a longer period of time. Which means you don't get a job. Plus I bet it's illegal to do this. Unless the bill itself is a charge for your writing up and mailing the bill to them.

12:21 P.M.

Forget About a Life of Crime

12:22 P.M.

Jealous of Birds and Squirrels and Dogs

Now that you've effectively left reality and anything productive in terms of a job search you might find yourself staring out the window. Out the window you might see birds and squirrels. You'll watch a bird sitting on a ledge watching the day go by. Or a friggin squirrel happily jumping from branch to branch. You also start to develop jealous feelings toward other animals. Animals don't have much responsibility and they can do what they want during the day without having outside pressures and stuff. Sometimes I'll look at a dog sitting there with a dumb dog look on his face and think, *I wonder if that dog knows how lucky he is. He gets patted on the head and he gets told "good job" just for like fetching a stick or sitting down. The only time*

JEALOUS

BIRD

JEALOUS OF BIRDS AND SQUIRRELS

SQUIRREL (DRAWN FROM MEMORY)

I ever got told "good job" at work was when I caught my boss's pencil as it rolled off his desk. He said, "Good job." Then he continued on and on about how I was underperforming.

But dogs don't underperform unless they're in the circus riding a trike. Cats and squirrels can do whatever they want all day too. They don't even have the distraction of conscious thought when they're sitting around doing nothing. Because they can't think. Squirrels might but cats don't. But when you sit around and do nothing . . . You get some thoughts sometimes. You get lots of thoughts. This separates our doing nothing from the animals' doing nothing.

P.S. If you're a cat owner who thinks that your cat thinks, I think you should think again about your cat thinking theory. Most likely, even your cat would think to disagree with you and your thoughts about it thinking . . . if it could think. Which I doubt it can. At least that's what I think about what you might be thinking.

12:32 P.M.

Genius Thought

Usually once a day I get like a genius thought. It floats in off the crest of some cosmic cloud and lands right in my melon head. Like this one genius idea I had was to start a Submarine Tour business that would circle Manhattan. I could picture people climbing down into the hatch and peering out the round windows on the side of the sub. I could serve drinks! And I could paint the sub to look like a whale wearing an I ♥ NY T-shirt, which would be cool. And tour around Manhattan like Circle Line but underwater. And people could look at the underside of Manhattan and see dead mobsters with cement shoes. And like sunken stuff and garbage and stuff. It would be a whole thing and touristy and weird. Genius?! No? Unfortunately, not genius. Someone told me that the rivers have so much muck that you couldn't see two feet in front of you. I thought about the sub having superspotlights but by then the motivation was killed. A single complication

can easily put the kibosh on a genius thought. Even though I'd still like to see it with my own eyes.

RULE #6: COMPLICATIONS DEMOTIVATE.

12:34 P.M.

Think About Moving to an Island

Eventually you might get fed up with the whole corporate world and the whole material possession thang and forgetting your best most geniusness thoughts. You might start looking around at where you are and what you're doing and decide you want to change your life altogether. You might be thinking to go move to some weirdo island or something or being a bartender. Or maybe getting a job at like Club Med and being the volleyball coach or limbo stick holder and all that.

Enough is enough with this nine to five stuff, right? Head down to an island and be like all relaxing in the sun all day and live in a hut! Sounds good, right? Become a pothead or whatever. It would be probably pretty excellent . . . for about a week. But if you live on a weirdo island, chances are you're going to want to come home pretty soon.

There's something about hanging out working while people are all vacationing right in your face that sucks. You gotta stare at some big fat guy

THIS
GUY

GO
USA!

who decides to wear a Speedo and dances around all drunk while you have to sit there with your finger on the blender all day long so he can go and have a good time right in your face? F that!

Being on an island wears off kind of fast just like it does when you're actually on vacation. Also the TV sucks. It's a known fact that on all islands they show only *Golden Girls* and *Mama's Family* and news on TV. That's it. And the news is all about what happened that day on *Mama's Family* or *Golden Girls.* After both of those shows got canceled and went into reruns the news itself became reruns too. So very soon TV on islands gets very old. Plus the reception sucks. On top of that the food is pretty off.

You'll long for your place and rainy days and lots of bad stuff to choose from on television. And the only person you have to make drinks for is you. So don't bother. But all this thinking about moving and stuff might make you a little hungry.

12:40 P.M.

Lunch

In the kitchen with Todd

Hungry? Yeah me too. All the time. It's a problem. I find the best way to manage this situation is to snack all day long. I find if I eat as much as possible I am often less hungry than if I restrict myself to three meals a day. Luckily due to the fact that my life has no regular structure it allows for this culinary flexibili-tay.

However I find that because of limited mon-ay and an overabundance of lack of motivation my shelves are often bare or down to the very basics with randomness here or there. Luckily this allows for alot of creativity in the kitchen.

Here are some recipes to inspire you to get creative in the kitchen:

FAKE EGGSHELL OMELETTE

INGREDIENTS: 4 EGGS
12 PRINGLES
BUTTER

BUTTER PAN AND COOK EGGS ANY WAY YOU DANG WELL PLEASE. THEN CRUNCH UP THE PRINGLES AND ADD THEM. MIX IT UP + SERVE. IT'S JUST LIKE THERE ARE EGG SHELLS IN THERE ... BUT WAY BETTER!

THAT SHOULD LOOK LIKE THIS HERE

LEFTOVER SHAKE AND BAKE

INGREDIENTS: LEFTOVERS
SALT

PREHEAT OVEN TO 350°. TAKE ALL YOUR LEFTOVERS OUT OF THE FRIDGE AND DUMP THEM OUT ON TINFOIL. THEN WRAP IT UP SO IT'S LIKE A BIG TIN DUMPLING. SHAKE IT UP. BAKE FOR 45 MINUTES.
* OPEN AWAY FROM FACE

CAP'N TODD'S CHEEZY TUNA SURPRISE

INGREDIENTS: 1 CAN TUNA
1 BOX MAC + CHEESE
1 CAN PEAS

MIX IT UP. IT'S GOOD!

CAP'N TODD'S CHEEZY TUNA SURPRISE

IT'S OK TO WRITE THE RECIPE ON THE BOWL. IT'S YOUR BOWL!

SORT OF A PIZZA-Y THINGEE

THAT RECIPE SHOULD LOOK LIKE THAT

* GREAT FOR INDISCRIMINATING GUESTS
INGREDIENTS: TOMATO SAUCE
CHEEZ WHIZ
WHEAT THINS

PREHEAT OVEN TO 350°. DUMP CRACKERS ON TIN FOIL. DUMP TOMATO SAUCE ON TOP OF THAT. SPRAY CHEEZ WHIZ ALL OVER THAT.

BAKE FOR 15 MINUTES. IF YOU WANNA GET FANCY WITH IT JUST SHAPE THE CRACKERS IN YOUR NAME OR FORM A CURSE WORD OR SOMETHING.

Butter-Corn-Butter POTATOES

INGREDIENTS: 2 POTATOES
1 STICK OF BUTTER
1 CAN CORN

BAKE OR MICROWAVE POTATOES TILL THEY'RE DONE. (I DON'T KNOW HOW LONG THAT TAKES.) SPLIT POTATOES. ADD ALOT OF BUTTER. DUMP CORN ON TOP. ADD THE REST OF THE BUTTER. SERVE W/ BEER GARNISH.

2 DORITO TUNA FISH CRUNCH SANDWICH

INGREDIENTS: BREAD
TUNA
DORITOS (COOL RANCH PREFERRED)

PREHEAT OVEN TO 350°. THEN PUT OUT 2 SLICES OF BREAD AND ADD TUNA THEN PUT DORITOS ON TOP OF THAT. ADD OTHER TWO SLICES OF BREAD. CRUNCH IT DOWN. SHUT OFF OVEN.

Don't like any of those? Make up your own dang recipe!

MAKE UP YER OWN RECIPE

TAKE ONE CAN OF _____ (FRUIT OR VEGETABLE)
MIX IN ONE BAG OF _____ (SNACK)
STIR IN A TEASPOON OF _____ (LIQUID)
SPRINKLE IN SOME _____ (POWDER)
MOLD IN THE SHAPE OF _____ (BODY PART)

BAKE AT _____ (NUMBER) DEGREES FOR _____ (NUMBER) (MEASURE OF TIME). WHEN DONE HOLD IT OVER YOUR _____ (BODY PART) AND SAY _____ (NONSENSE WORD)!
GARNISH WITH _____ (SOMETHING GREEN)
CALL IT: _____ (ANIMAL) _____ (SAUCE) _____ (COLOR)

Exercise

You may find after lying around doing nothing and snacking on junk food you have a voice in your head telling you to get off your ass and run around the block or something. I hear this voice often. I call him Yapper. He tells me to do alot of stuff. I've learned to try and ignore him. Sometimes I mock Yapper in my own pretend voice. Like if Yapper in my head says, "Hey tubby, how about laying off the ice cream? You're looking pretty roundish," I'll eat a glob of a triple scoop sundae with rainbow sprinkles and say back in a high-pitched whiny voice while chewing, "Hey tubby, how about laying off the ice cream? You're looking pretty roundish." And then eat another glob.

But occasionally Yapper gets through a little and I decide to accept that occasionally he may have a point. Granted Yapper also

THIS IS YAPPER
(ARTIST RENDITION. NOT AN ACTUAL PHOTO.)

told me dot-coms were a great career move and that credit cards are completely different than spending cash.

Anyway, when Yapper nags me alot about exercise sometimes I do what he says just to get him to shut up. I think if Yapper was a chick voice I'd probably do stuff without as much of a fight. But if you're a chick with a guy Yapper my guess is you argue every suggestion.

So here are some samples of exercises that you might want to try at home just to quiet your own Yapper. All have a low risk factor due to the fact that you might not have health insurance and if you drop a weight on your head or something you're going to feel doubly stupid.

Exercises You Might Want to Try at Home

REMOTE CONTROL RELAY

Leave your remote control on top of your television set. Your watching TV will become a ten-foot dash all day long. It might be annoying after a while but it works. You can set the various resistance levels just by moving your chair closer or farther away from the TV.

ON YOUR MARK...
GET SET

M&M DISASTER EXERCISE

Buy yourself one of those big one-pound bags of M&Ms (peanut preferred because they roll crazier). Yank open the bag in a way that the M&Ms explode all over the place. Then go fetch em up. You'll be crawling around. Moving furniture. Going all over the place for like an hour. The best part about this is you end up with a whole bowl full of M&Ms to eat when you're done.

BIG WHEEL CIRCLES

Get an old Big Wheel from your parents' house or eBay or something. Bring it home and clear out the biggest room you have. Get a pair of swim goggles and a crash helmet. Hop on the Big Wheel. Start off by pedaling slowly then increase speed over time until you're going at a good clip. Concentrate on doing as many donuts as you can before you wipe out. Then after you wipe out pick the Big Wheel up over your head and run around in circles declaring victory.

NEIGHBOR FIGHT

Getting in a fight with your neighbor is a good way to get exercise. First pick your biggest neighbor. Then depending on where you live there's a few things you can do to make him want to fight. Spray him in the face with a hose. Walk on his car with cleats. Steal his mailbox. Huck an egg at him. Write your name on his door. Talk about his wife or girlfriend in a negatively sexual way. Then run away back into your apartment and shut the door almost all the way. Your neighbor will try and barge his way in. You push back and try to keep the door closed. This is a good workout. If the neighbor gets in it gets even better. This exercise is not recommended for chicks as guys interpret this behavior as flirting.

YOUR NEW WORKOUT BUDDY

WALKING ON YOUR HANDS

Most likely you cannot walk on your hands but you can try and teach yourself. This will be exercise. Make sure you clear a good amount of space in your place before attempting this. Being upside down and then falling onto your back

hitting your spine against the corner of a table . . . sucks. Also do not do this right after you eat a bowl of M&Ms. Throwing up while upside down will end this workout. Don't do this naked either for a variety of reasons but the number one reason is none of us looks good standing on our heads naked. But if you're a chick and beg to differ, feel free to send me a photo.

PLAY ROCK STAR

This is always good for a good workout. Get yourself a tennis racket and you too can be just like Nikki Sixx in your head. Make sure you jump around alot and do spins and stuff. If you're looking for an extended workout just crank up the speakers to 10 and combine this workout with Neighbor Fight.

(SHUT THE BLINDS BEFORE PERFORMING THIS EXERCISE.)

← SUPERBALL

SUPERBALL BOUNCY

Bounce a SuperBall around. It's good for your reflexes. Act like a cat.

(BOUNCY.)

Exercises You Should Not Attempt

LIFTING WEIGHTS

I have experimented with weights and I have found them to be quite heavy and often you have to strain, especially if you do this for an extended period of time. Also after a workout sometimes you feel very sore, which can't be good for you. In general everything associated with weights is uncomfortable.

JOGGING

I attempted jogging once. I got all decked out in my tennis shoes and shorts and went running down the street. By the time I got to the end of the block I was very winded and I felt a little silly for running down the street. Somehow I couldn't distinguish between "exercise" and "running down the street like a dick." I walked home and napped for two hours solid after that workout.

YOGA

I found out that 100 percent of all people want to do yoga. It seems right for everyone. Minimal exercise. Healthy feeling. You get to see chicks bend around and stuff. Or if you're a chick you can have yoga guys feel you up pretending they're "helping with that position." But often yoga classes are in the morning so this does not fit into your schedule. And you'll also find out soon enough that yoga is boring. Plus, the one time I tried it, I farted alot and fell over into a wall and pretty much humiliated myself.

OTHER EXERCISE POSSIBILITIES

I can't play basketball cause I can't go left. I can't play baseball cause I can't keep my eye on the ball. I can't play golf cause I can't afford it. Same with skiing. I can't play beach volleyball cause I have backhair. I can't walk the dog cause I don't have a dog. I can't have sex cause I have no one to have sex with except me and that's hardly a workout. Also I can't boccie ball cause I don't know how. Ping-Pong gets on my nerves and I usually smush the ball before the end of the match and run away crying. I can't play sports in general for the most part due to the uncoordination thing. But that's just me.

2:03 P.M.
Doing Other Stuff

Unfortunately the Yapper who tells you to exercise might sometimes convince you to do other stuff. This may interfere with your doing nothing properly. Oftentimes Yapper will cause you to get "ambitious." If you feel this coming on try and lie down to relax. If you can't shake it I would say you should go with it as it will be a distraction till it is out of your system. I won't stand in the way of your ambitions but just realize that being ambitious usually involves work. And if it leads to anything it will lead to more work. I know this for a fact as you can tell by the fact that you are reading this book. Writing this book totally ruined my doing nothing time for an extended period of time. Here are some things that may come up that you might want to try when you feel ambitious:

Writing a Screenplay

I found out that it's kind of difficult to write a screenplay for a number of reasons. But the main reason is that they're easy to start and hard to get past page 2. I've started a bunch of them.

Like I started one about this chick who started receiving postcards in the mail from across the country from someone who never signed his name. At first they were flirty and then they got scary . . . and scarier. And she noticed the postmarks of the cities were getting closer and closer as the messages got scarier and scarier. He was crossing the country heading toward her. She could tell by the postmarks. Until they were coming from her own city. Scary right? Then . . . then . . .

Then I couldn't figure out who was sending the postcards or why so I forgot about that and tried another one.

The mov-ay opens with the camera following a pigeon flying over New York City. We see an overhead view of the buildings and the bird flying. The bird makes a poop and we follow the poop rocketing down falling between the buildings past the windows zooming down to the street till it plunks down in a cup of coff-ay on the street. The owner of the cup stirs it up with a plastic straw and takes a sip. He didn't notice the birdpoop. We see he's a detective standing at a crime scene. There is a box on the street filled with lopped-off arms and on the box it says A FAREWELL TO ARMS. "Hell of a city," the detective says then takes another sip. I'm not sure what happens after that but I got lots of intros.

The Writing Part

If you want to get started on your script but don't know where to get started—keep in mind that there have only been ten mov-ays made in the history of film. Just change the names and the location. Here are the ten:

1. Naive nice guy gets too involved with a sophisticated bad girl. Add mayhem. During the summer.
2. Aliens come. We win.
3. It's war. Hero dies. Sidekick lives with guilt.
4. It's arty. There's a strange character in a strange world. Weird stuff happens. In the end it turns out that he caused it all. And dreams were reality. (Not recommended due to poor box-office performance.)
5. Evil business plan. Young exec finds out about it and has to make a moral decision. Questions himself. Wimps out and blows the whistle. This sometimes takes place in the future all sci-fi.
6. Dog talks.
7. Killer on the loose. Kills someone close to the main detective or whatever. Turns out the killer is a close friend. Killer gets killed in the end either by gunshot or dropped off building or cliff. Sometimes arrested if cop Pussies out.
8. Take foreigner. Put in another country. Have him deal awkwardly with new customs. Ends up a hero for the country.
9. Guy meets girl. They do it. But something goes all wrong. Sometimes happy ending but sometimes not. Add music.
10. Take franchise character. Make another sequel. Beat to death. Repeat.

The Selling Part

Once you put your mind to it it's not so hard to write a whole mov-ay. The hard part is like selling it. Most likely when you send a script to Hollywood it ends up in the equivalent of a dead letter office. But here are some ways to bring attention to yourself if you head to Hollywood to sell a script.

- Put on a one-man or one-woman show on Hollywood Boulevard acting out all the parts of your mov-ay by yourself. Sort of like a one-man-band-type deal except not. This is especially good if you have written a script that's full of action or sex. You must act out all the scenes and do the sound effects yourself to "keep it real."

- Show up at the mov-ay studio gate and throw your script into the sunroofs of cars that drive into the lot. Aim for the head. Most execs don't respond to anything unless it hits them over the head.
- Most people in Hollywood are insecure about everything so it's best to take advantage of that. If you do happen to get a script into the hands of some producers or something just say "[Insert rival producer's name here] has already offered me two hundred and fifty K for the rights. But I'm not sure .. .." They'll know it's a lie but then you're speaking their language and they respect that. (By the way, if there are any Hollywood people reading this right now and you're like all offended by what I'm saying I really don't mean it. I'm one of you but I'm just playing up to the "real people" to keep it real and stuff. Wink wink.)
- Make Hollywood people believe you're an authentic person. One of the "real people" and not some Hollywood phony. But you have to be smart enough to show that you know how the game works.

Writing a Children's Book

Writing a book for kids seems like an easy way to make a living. You just write a bunch of dopey things, draw some pictures, and then some publisher sends you a check and orders like five more books or something. This is actually one of the projects I did finish and I put it in the book! Which is cool cause if you're a mom or dad hanging out doing nothing and your brat . . . I mean kid comes over to you while you're on the couch reading this and needs to be entertained, you don't even have to get your ass off the couch!

Just turn the page and read em this . . .

ELF UP! AND MEP!
QUEST FOR ☆MAGIC

by
odd todd

ONE DAY ELF UP DECIDED HE WANTED
TO QUEST FOR MAGIC.
HE VISITED HIS FRIEND MEP TO SEE IF
MEP KNEW WHERE THEY COULD FIND MAGIC.
MEP LOOKED UP AT THE CEILING AND SAID, "MEP."
BECAUSE MEP DIDN'T BELIEVE IN MAGIC.
AFTER ALL, MEP WAS A MEP...

ELF
UP!

-MEP!

BUT ELF UP CONVINCED MEP TO
JOIN HIM ON THE QUEST FOR MAGIC.
"ELF UP!" ELF UP SAID CHEERILY
EXCITED FOR SOME MAGIC.
"MEP," MEP SAID NOT SO CHEERILY THINKING
THIS WAS GOING TO BE A BIG WASTE OF TIME.

THEY FIRST WENT TO VISIT TV TURTLE.

"ELF UP!" SAID ELF UP
(ASKING TV TURTLE IF HE KNEW
    WHERE TO FIND SOME MAGIC).

BUT TV TURTLE WAS TOO BUSY WITH
TV TO THINK ABOUT MAGIC. HIS FAVORITE
SHOW CALLED "SHELLY'S SEASHELL"
WAS COMING ON SOON AND HE DIDN'T
WANT TO MISS IT.

"MEP," SAID MEP. MEP DIDN'T LIKE
THAT TV SHOW. MEP ONLY LIKED
GAME SHOWS.

THEIR NEXT STOP WAS AT DELI BIRD'S...

"ELF UP!" SAID ELF UP
(ASKING DELI BIRD ABOUT MAGIC).

BUT DELI BIRD WAS TOO BUSY MAKING
A SANDWICH TO THINK ABOUT MAGIC.
DELI BIRD WAS MAKING AN ONION, CHEDDAR
CHEESE, AND MUSTARD SANDWICH.

"MEP," SAID MEP. MEP DIDN'T LIKE ONIONS.
HE DIDN'T LIKE CHEDDAR CHEESE OR
MUSTARD MUCH EITHER.

THE NEXT STOP WAS KING BLOB'S . . .

"ELF UP!" SAID ELF UP
(ASKING KING BLOB ABOUT MAGIC).

BUT KING BLOB WAS TOO BUSY
THINKING BLOBBY THOUGHTS AND DOING
BLOBBY THINGS AND MAKING UP BLOBBY
RULES.

"MEP," SAID MEP. MEP DIDN'T LIKE
BLOBBY THOUGHTS OR BLOBBY THINGS.

AND CERTAINLY DIDN'T LIKE ANY
BLOBBY RULES...

THE NEXT STOP WAS THE LADYBUG HIDEOUT...

BUT IT WAS TEA TIME AT THE LADYBUG
HIDEOUT AND DURING TEA TIME AT THE
LADYBUG HIDEOUT LADYBUGS ONLY LIKED
TO TALK ABOUT TEA AND THE COLOR RED.
NOT MAGIC.

"ELF UP?" SAID ELF UP WORRIED THAT THEY
WEREN'T GOING TO FIND ANY MAGIC.

"MEP," SAID MEP.
MEP WANTED A MEP HIDEOUT FOR MEPS.

THE NEXT STOP WAS
DR. AND MRS. STOMP STOMPS.

THE STOMP STOMPS WERE TOO BUSY
STOMPING AROUND TO THINK ABOUT MAGIC.
BUT MRS. STOMP STOMP ASKED IF MEP AND
ELF UP WANTED TO JOIN THEM IN A STOMP.

"ELF UP..." SAID ELF UP.

(THANKING THEM FOR THE INVITATION TO
STOMP WITH THEM. BUT THEY HAD TO
BE ON THEIR WAY BECAUSE ...)

"MEP!!" MEP INTERRUPTED ANGRILY.
(MEP LOVED TO STOMP AND HE WASN'T
GOING ANYWHERE UNTIL THEY DID SOME
                        STOMPING!)

SO ELF UP AND MEP WENT OFF STOMP STOMPING WITH DR. AND MRS. STOMP STOMP

THEY STOMPED
THE MUD

THEY STOMPED
THE ROCKS

THEY STOMPED
A STICK

THEY STOMPED
THE DIRT

THEY STOMPED
THE WATER

THEY EVEN
STOMPED THE
AIR

THEY DID ALOT OF STOMPING. EVENTUALLY ELF UP
AND MEP GOT VERY TIRED . . .

THEY TOOK A BREAK FROM STOMPING AND
SAT DOWN ON A COMFY HILL UNDER A SUNNY SKY.

"ELF UP?" SAID ELF UP
(ASKING MEP WHAT KEPT THE CLOUDS IN THE SKY).
"MEP," SAID MEP SHRUGGING HIS MEP SHOULDERS.

"ELF UP?" SAID ELF UP WHILE LOOKING AT A FLOWER.
(HE WANTED TO KNOW WHAT MADE THE FLOWERS GROW).

"MEP," SAID MEP SHAKING HIS MEP HEAD.

"ELF UP?" SAID ELF UP WATCHING A BUTTERFLY FLY BY.
(HE WANTED TO KNOW HOW CATERPILLARS BECAME
BUTTERFLIES).

"MEP!" SAID MEP ROLLING HIS MEP EYES. MEP DIDN'T
KNOW THAT EITHER. AFTER ALL MEP WAS ONLY A MEP.

"ELF UP..." ELF UP SAID QUIETLY.
(ELF UP THOUGHT IT MIGHT ALL BE MAGIC).

MEP WAS QUIET FOR A WHILE AS HE
 LOOKED UP AT THE SKY.
"MEP," SAID MEP NODDING HIS MEP HEAD.

"MEP," MEP SAID AGAIN.
(AGREEING IT MIGHT INDEED BE...MAGIC).

AND MAYBE IT WAS...

THE TWO FRIENDS STARED UP AT THE SKY WELL
AFTER THE SUN WENT DOWN. THEY WONDERED
ABOUT THE MOON AND SHOOTING STARS AND
AND NOISES IN THE DARK AND THE RAIN.

THEY FELL ASLEEP THINKING ABOUT THE SUN RISING
AND REALIZED THEY SAW MAGIC EVERYWHERE
THEY LOOKED...

AND THEY KNEW THEY WOULD SEE MORE MAGIC TOMORROW
AND TOMORROW'S TOMORROW. AND THE TOMORROW
AFTER THAT.

"MEP!" SAID MEP WHILE TALKING IN HIS SLEEP. HE
SOUNDED HAPPY.

"ELF UP..." ELF UP SAID. HE SMILED BIG AND FELL
ASLEEP EXCITED FOR THE MAGIC THAT DREAMS
WILL BRING...

Writing children's books or screenplays and stuff might get you thinking about a total career change. Luckily, I've thought alot about this stuff. So while you're feeling motivated you might as well explore a few alternative careers. You'll find that most of them seem to involve a minimal amount of work and a maximum amount of mon-ay and recognition.

Being a Mov-Ay Star

You might be inclined to decide to be a mov-ay star. Being a mov-ay star seems totally cool. You hang out on mov-ay sets and collect big checks. People follow you around with stuff you like, like Fritos or Fresca. Whatever you tell them to follow you around with. You can get addicted to stuff and it actually helps your career. The problem with trying to be a mov-ay star is the chances are one step above winning the lottery. The easier path to being a mov-ay star is by buying a lottery ticket and winning. Then buy your own mov-ay and put yourself in it. Give yourself a supporting actor role as someone who is mentally disturbed. That way you can win an Oscar. Don't worry about talent. No mov-ay stars have any real talent.

—MEP!

MOV-AY STAR

BiTHER ASSISTANT WITH BAG OF STUFF

If you plan to be a mov-ay star you can practice yelling at your assistant with this here Mad Lib.

HEY! _____ (UNINTELLIGENT PERSON) _____ (CURSE WORD) FACE!

I ASKED YOU __ (SMALL NUMBER) MINUTES AGO FOR

A _____ (BRAND OF SODA)! AND YOU BRING ME THIS

_____ (BRAND OF SODA)?! IT TASTES LIKE _____ (ZOO ANIMAL)

_____ (BODY SECRETION)! AND DON'T JUST STAND THERE

LIKE A _____ (STUPID PERSON) PICK UP THAT _____ (OFFICE SUPPLY)!

NOW LICK IT! NOW STICK IT IN YOUR

_____ (BODY ORIFICE)! YOU _____ (CURSE ADJECTIVE) _____ (CURSE WORD) _____ (ZOO ANIMAL)!

AND GET THAT LITTLE _____ (SLANG/SEX ORGAN) HEAD

_____ (CURSE) _____ (MOVIE STAR) ON THE PHONE NOW!

BY THE WAY, THAT _____ (ARTICLE OF CLOTHING) YOU'RE

WEARING MAKES YOU LOOK LIKE A _____ (LARGE ZOO ANIMAL)!!

Open a Bar

Opening a bar seems cool. You get to hang out in a bar all day and eat wings and stuff. There are a few problems with opening a bar. The main problem is mon-ay. You need sort of alot of it to get started. Not only to open the bar but also to bribe the city officials and mobsters and stuff. Opening a bar involves so much work that by the time you open the bar you're already sick of it. Plus your bar atmosphere can go all sorts of ways cause of the clientele. A friend of mine opened a beer bar and the customers were not what he expected. Now he has to dress all goth to fit in to his own stupid bar. He's totally bummed. My suggestion is to hang out in a bar for a week straight. At the end of that week if you still feel like opening a bar go for it. But you won't.

Speaking of bars here's a few drinking games you can play while just sitting around watching TV thinking about opening a bar.

SITCOM DRINKING

Sit yourself down with a bunch of beers and watch a sitcom. Drink at these points:

- You see nipples through a shirt.
- Someone gives someone a look.
- You get annoyed at someone.
- Anyone eats or drinks anything.
- Someone says, "Hey."
- Someone touches someone else.
- Someone doesn't understand what the other one is talking about.

Time to chug: Someone walks in or out of a room.

BASEBALL DRINKING

Drink at these points:

- The announcer announces the count.
- Someone takes a practice swing.
- They zoom in on someone in the crowd.
- Someone spits.
- The catcher catches the pitch.

Time to chug: Foul ball!

COMMERCIAL DRINKING

If you want to take it a little easy only drink during commercials. You'll find that when you have no mon-ay commercials are extra annoying because absolutely nothing is directed at you. You are not part of any target market. Drink at these points:

- Every time someone on TV tells *you* what *you* will love.
- Every time a company does something "creative" with its logo.
- Every time there is an ad for a product that is in a bottle.

Time to chug: Whenever there is an ad for a product that doesn't apply to you.

Inventing Something

A really good get-rich-quick thing is to invent something and patent it. I've thought of a few things along the way. Like the "Mailbox Alert," which was a buzzer that would go off in your house when the mail carrier put mail in your mailbox. I thought this would be cool for people who were really into their mail. Someone else thought the same thing and patented it first. Bastard stole my idea totally. The other thing that I wanted to patent was a little more stupid. What I thought of was like a mirror with an arm attached to a headband for back shaving. You wear it on your head in the shower and can look at your back. I found out I was alone in wanting this invention. A rule of thumb with patents: If you're the only person who will want your idea it's probably not worth patenting.

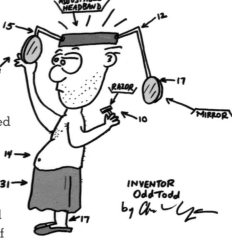

THE MIRROR HEADBAND BACK SHAVER THING
(PATENT #470321940)

ADJUSTABLE HEADBAND

15
12
44
RAZOR
17
MIRROR
10
14
31
17

INVENTOR
Odd Todd
by Ch~~~~

Starting a Band

Being a rock star is also a coolio idea. It seems like a pretty groovy way to pay the bills. This unfortunately did not work out for me because when I tried guitar I found out I can't have my left hand do anything different than my right hand. I tried to learn "Stairway to Heaven" but I really couldn't figure it out. When I tried bass guitar it seemed all backward. And when I tried drums I found out I could do a single steady beat pretty well but when I tried like cymbals or something it threw everything off. Then the guy in the music store threw me out. Then the band broke up.

Understanding Your Yapper

Although Yapper pushes you to do things he's an interesting character cause as soon as he gets you doing stuff he'll immediately turn on you and make fun of you for doing whatever it is you've decided to do. Yapper will tell you you're being silly. That you're wasting your time. That you're no good at it. That you're dreaming. This is when you need to tune out Yapper. If you're doing something it's for a reason and go with it. Stick with it!

Or don't . . . whatever.

YOU'RE BEING SILLY. GIVE UP!

YEAH RIGHT... YOU CAN'T DO THAT

DON'T BOTHER JUST SIT ON THE COUCH WITH YOUR OLD FRIEND YAPPER

YOU DON'T HAVE IT IN YOU.

It's too LATE TO START.

IF YOU WERE REALLY GOING TO DO THAT YOU WOULD HAVE DONE IT ALREADY!

*BEWARE OF YAPPER! HE CAN TURN ON YOU AND TELL YOU LIES.

Naptime

All this thinking about stuff will make you sleepy. Plus you've accomplished alot today. You got up. Made coff-ay. Job searched. Ate some snacks. It's time to lie down for a quick powernap.

RULE #7: NAPS ARE KEY FOR SANITY AND GOOD HEALTH.

Location, location, location.

These are the three words essential to napping. You probably have two choices when thinking about napping. The bed or the couch. Naps are meant for the couch. Something about getting back in bed seems wrong. If you get in bed at 2:32 for a nap you might end up sleeping until like 6:00. This would be bad cause when you wake up you'll feel all nutty. Like you'll look around the room and have no idea what day it is or what time it is. Sometimes you won't even know where the hell you are or what year it is. This is bad cause overcoming this amnesia is not doing nothing . . . it's overcoming amnesia.

My suggestion is napping on the couch. If necessary feel free to take a pillow and light blankee with you to the couch to maximize comfort but do not get back into bed. If you have a stuffed animal, that can join you as well.

Nap Techniques

THE FACE PLANT

The way this is accomplished is for you to get up on your knees on one end of the couch. Then toss the pillow to the other end of the couch. Allow yourself to fall facefirst into the pillow and keep your arms at your sides. This is also referred to in the espionage world as "POS"—pass out simulation. When international spies need to convince the enemy that they're passing out they will "Pull a POS." Make sure you have enough clearance so you don't whomp your head on the arm of the couch. Although you'll most likely nap immediately if you do that.

THE FACE PLANT

63

THE SIT-UP NAP

THE SIT-UP

This is another good nap technique. Here's how it's done:

Lie down on the couch on your back and interlace your fingers behind your head. And then do a sit-up. Touch your elbows to your knees. Then lie back down again. This most likely will give you a bigger appreciation for the fact that you're lying down and not doing sit-ups. Plus doing that single sit-up will most likely soak up the rest of the energy you have, which allows you to ease into nappy-nap land. If necessary go for the second sit-up but this should be utilized only in an extreme situation. You don't want to strain yourself prior to napping.

FRENCH NAPPING

THE FRENCH NAP

Originated around 1754 by King Louis XIV this nap technique has a tragic history. Louis was a big fan of napping and insisted all the people in the country nap at the same time during the day. He felt this was a safety precaution as, if everyone napped during the day at the same time, nobody could sneak up on him and dethrone him. Everyone would be too busy napping to deal with the dethroning. He also insisted that everyone nap naked too because if people did awake from a nap they would have no weapons on them to run up and stab him with. At first this worked out great and everyone enjoyed their daily nap. However, Attila the Hun found out about this French nap technique and he invaded France during naptime. The French were all naked and caught off guard completely. They bravely tried to fight while naked but their slaps and kicks were nothing compared to the heavily armored Hun. The French were not liberated from Attila the Hun until 1977.

But if you decide to French Nap (aka naked napping): Make sure you lock your doors and shut the windows in case of an invasion. And get naked!

THE GOPHER

The trick to this one is to imagine you're a gopher down in your gopher hole. Lie down on the couch and burrow yourself into the crease of the couch. Get in there as tight as you can and cover yourself with a blanket. Make sure you can breathe cause not breathing interferes with proper napping. Get it in your head that you are a gopher. Think gophery thoughts. Shrug your shoulders into position in a gophery way. You're underground. Safe in your hole. Make sure you're on your side. Dig in. Fade out. You'll awaken in dreamland covered in fur with buck teeth.

3:26 P.M.

Postnap Activities

Ok . . . you're awake again. Feel refreshed? A little groggy most likely. Here are some things to do to help jumpstart your brain.

Jumpstart Your Brain

CEILING AND BALL GAME

Take a tennis ball or something and lie on your back and throw it toward the ceiling. See how close you can get the ball to the ceiling without the ball actually touching the ceiling. If the ball touches the ceiling then start over again.

EYE RUB FIREWORKS

If you rub your eyes really hard eventually you'll start to generate colors on the backs of your eyelids. It's sort of like a fireworks display just for you. To enhance the effect feel free to make the *"boom!"* and *"baboom!"* noises. Also *"Pow!"*

Eye Rub Fireworks are terrific!

EYE RUB FIREWORKS LOOK LIKE THIS SOMETIMES

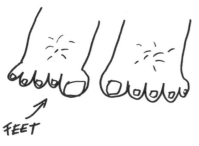

FEET

(MY LACK OF FORMAL ART TRAINING IS DEMONSTRATED HERE)

LOOK AT YOUR FEET

This is a nice activity too. Sometimes days go by without my looking at my feet. They're weird looking with the toes and weird baby nail. The big toes look like thumbs. They're really marvels of human physiology. Great in so many ways. At one point you might be horrified by your toenails. At this point you should stop looking at your feet. Girls almost never like their feet so this is not recommended.

PRANK CALL

It's fun to prank call friends while they're at work. Depending on the business they're in you can trick them totally. Call them up in a grumbly voice and when they pick up ask them why they didn't call you back. When they don't know what you're talking about get all offended that not only did they not call you back but they don't even remember you at all. Ask to talk to their boss. Throw a mini-tantrum. Tell them you had doubts about dealing with them in the first place. And now those doubts are confirmed. Demand to talk to their boss. Listen to your friends stutter and squirm. Then start laughing. At this point they'll probably hang up on you.

Other Ways to Bug People at Work Over the Phone

Call them up and:

- Say, "Jeez man where the hell are you? We've been waiting fifteen minutes in the conference room!"
- Tell them that you just applied for their job. Tell them you thought it was weird when you saw it advertised on Monster.
- Tell their assistants secrets about them. And old nicknames.
- Tell them you're ripped drunk and coming over to tell them off because of what they did. Then hang up. Sound very drunk.
- Tell them how you're having a crisis and can't decide between a nap and going to sit in the park.
- Call them every two minutes with panicked reports about the soap opera you're watching.
- Shove potato chips in your mouth and mumble stuff. When they say "What?" shove more chips in your mouth and mumble louder.
- Arrange a conference call with them and the take-out order taker at the Chinese restaurant.
- Tell them how if you want to you can call their boss at any time and say crazy shit.
- Ask them what they're doing. Then tell them what you're doing.

Take a Shower

The midafternoon shower is great for a number of reasons. For me it's great cause it ensures hot water. In my building if you try and shower between 8:00 and 9:00 A.M. there is a chance you'll run out of hot water. If this happens to you, you might end up groping around for a towel to clear the shampoo out of your eyes. I fortunately don't have this problem cause I don't have shampoo. Cause I don't have hair. I think everyone is paranoid that their hair is falling out all the time.

The morning shower is tough cause it's a shock to the system. People who have to go to work take showers to shock themselves awake. The kind of life you're living does not need shock. You want to ease into your day.

Also sometimes you get upset with what you see and you don't want to upset yourself first thing in the morning. I like to feel my gut and wonder about it. Wonder if it was that big yesterday. It seemed smaller yesterday somehow. It must be my imagination. Then I wonder where all the cook-ays went. I find women can look at their bodies and find things wrong with every aspect of their bodies if they try hard enough. That's why it's best not to focus on yourself in the shower. You women have to stop it with that. You have boobs. Big or small. It doesn't matter. Case closed.

NO SHOWERING IN THE MORNING

67

Luckily there's other stuff to do in the shower to distract you from your hair and your belly. There's some things you might want to take in the shower with you.

FOUR FRICKIN FUN ACTIVITIES FOR THE SHOWER

WEAR SOCKS
(MAKE FUN WET SLAPPY NOISES ON BOTTOM OF TUB)

WEAR A SHOWERCAP
(SELF EXPLANATORY)

BRING IN A CAT AND TRY TO TICKLE IT

DRAW PICTURE OF A BIG PENIS.

♪ ... ALSO
SING!
♫ SING!
♫ SING IN THE
SHOWER!!

HERE ARE SOME SONGS I LIKE TO SING:

GARTH BROOKS - FRIENDS IN LOW PLACES
BEATLES - TICKET TO RIDE
DAVID BOWIE - MODERN LOVE
FRANK SINATRA - SUMMER WIND
BANANA SPLITS THEME SONG
WELCOME BACK KOTTER THEME SONG
JACKSON BROWNE - SOMEBODY'S BABY
MOTLEY CRUE - LOOKS THAT KILL
THE TUBES - SHE'S A BEAUTY
NELLY - HOT IN HERRE

Bath?

Of course, you could take a bath but baths don't usually work out for me. It seems like it takes forever to fill up the tub and when you have a short attention span you can wander away and go play a video game or something and end up flooding your place. Flooding your place sucks because first you've got to clean up all the water, which is "work" but also it can leak through the floor into the apartment downstairs and you're not on good terms with that guy because he's always complaining about your frickin music and asking if you "walk around in high heels all day" and he'll like come pounding on your door telling you to turn down your "frickin TV game show." And you stare at the door all quiet and scared cause he seems crazy. But then again there are benefits to getting your neighbor all mad as we already know.

I find that chicks can sit there all day splashing around or doing whatever. But for me, within like two minutes I'm hot. I don't fit in the tub right and am uncomfortable. The drain noise is annoying. I have to pee. I drop my book in the water. I slosh water out of the tub on the floor. It's like f— it.

Other Postnap Activities

FANTASIZE ABOUT WINNING THE LOTTERY

I think alot about winning the lottery. I wouldn't be all selfish with it either. I'd like be charitable and help my friends. (Hear that gods of good luck??) But I'd also buy some stuff for me. I'd buy alot of stuff to help the economy.

Here's some stuff I'd buy:

THINGS I'D BUY IF I WIN THE LOTTERY

-EEP.

MONKEY

TRIP TO OUTERSPACE

BOOBS IN FACE ALARM CLOCK

A REALLY GOOD SHOWERHEAD

♥ + ☺
LOVE + HAPPINESS
(I KNOW...
BUT I'D GIVE
IT MY BEST SHOT)

THE POWER OF INVISIBILITY

THE PRINGLES FACTORY

THE 51st STATE TODAOKA

ANTEATER AND ANTS

APPRECIATING YOUR NEWFOUND FREEDOM

Besides screwing around and throwing a ball around and showering there's alot of other things that you can do when you have your days to yourself. You can kill hours playing video games. You can stand up with a bag of popcorn and play catch with the popcorn and your mouth. You can make up dance moves. You can look at yourself naked in the mirror from all different angles. You can look up words. You can make like those orange juice Popsicles in an ice tray with toothpicks. You can start to think about what to do next. You can start to worry about a couple of things. You can . . . you can . . .

3:54 P.M.

Have a Panic Attack

Now that you've napped and showered and snacked and spaced out you might feel your mind wander around in your head. Sometimes your mind gets stupid and makes you think about important stuff like:

Credit Card Debt

If you're like me you've managed to work up a nice hefty amount of debt. You may have gone into this phase where you felt like, *I deserve those things.* Then that might have moved into, *Well I'm going to buy these things eventually . . . why not just buy them now?* Then you went into this phase where somehow credit cards were not the same as mon-ay and you did a little spending spree.

CREDIT CARD
DEBT SUCKS

Then you decided that you would get a bonus from work and you would pay everything off but then getting the bonus made you celebrate and you spent it all and sent Visa like five hundred dollars just to "feel responsible." Then you said, *Well I'm already in debt! What's another couple thousand gonna hurt?* Then you said, *I can always go bankrupt. That's like setting the meter back to zero, right?*

Now you're here. With a serious credit card situation. This is when Yapper may pay you a visit. He crawls up your back and sits down on your shoulder. Pretty much minding his own business but then he whispers in your ear, "Way to go. You had to be a big shot, didja?"

Job Worries

All of a sudden while you're still absorbing the credit card situation you start thinking about your job situation (or lack thereof). You can't believe that things have turned out the way they are. The last time you looked at your résumé it looked dated and your experience seemed ridiculous. Lots of the companies you dealt with have gone out of business and you don't trust the people you used to rely on for references. The last few résumés you sent out went out into the black hole of cyberspace and all the people you used to network with are looking for new jobs too. You're seriously considering looking into jobs that offer like a 50 percent cut from the salary you once had. Interviewers ask if you're "comfortable" with that. And you might even be lucky to get that.

Now you're here with no career. Or a career you don't like. And no real prospects.

Yapper seems to have grown a bit. Once a little thing sitting on your shoulder he's now like sitting on both your shoulders kicking his feet and rocking and giving you annoying wet willies in your ears.

Yapper then says in your ear in a more confident voice, "Don't worry man, you can always move home with Mom and Dad."

Moving Home with Mom and Dad

Mom and Dad have hopefully been supportive in keeping their doors open for you if push comes to shove. And it would take a hell of a shove to get you packing your stuff up and moving home. Most likely that shove would come from your landlord. Moving home with Mom and Dad would most likely suck big-time but if you gotta do it you gotta do it. Life can be worse. But the idea of bumping into your neighbors and driving around the old neighborhood and running into high school friends and all that is the real issue. That would suck big-time. You might save money but you'd definitely pay a bit of a price, right?

Yapper sees his opening and goes for it. He swings over your head and holds on to your ears. He looks you straight in the face and gives you a big kiss.

And then says in rapid fire:

*Rent-Healthinsurance-Debt-Lovelife-Thatsuspiciousmole-youregetting
old-youregoingcrazy-generalhealth-terrorismiscoming-duck-chemicals-
addictionsaremounting-pressure-obsessivecompulsive-nervousbreak-
down-gettingfat-lackingtalent-losinghair-irresponsible-alcoholism-you
willendinguplivingonthestreetinaboxandyoubumpintoanoldhighschool-
friendandhegivesyoualookandyourecognizeeachotherandthenyoucrawl-
backintoyourboxandyouheartheoldfriendgentlyplacesomechangeontop
ofyourbox/house.*

And before you know it your heart starts picking up speed and you can't clear the thoughts out of your head. You can't even latch on to one thought in particular but it's an overall vibe. The blizzard of negative thought is white noise in your head. Eventually it covers everything and Yapper is jumping up and down on your head screaming, "Go! Go! *Go!!*"

I found there is a good way to get Yapper off of you for a little while . . .

4:12 P.M.

Television

RULE #8: TELEVISION IS GOOD.

Here's why:

First off it immediately fills your head with nonsense that's better than the nonsense Yapper puts in your head. In general, it helps get rid of Yapper. Well, it doesn't really get "rid of" Yapper. It's more like Yapper itself gets distracted by the TV and sits down with you on the couch to watch a few shows. Sometimes it's good to watch TV while hanging your head off the couch upside down. This makes negative flow of thought drain properly.

Over time the importance of television grows and grows. You can judge the level of importance by arranging what order you will stop paying bills in. Here's my list from most important to least important:

TOP TEN BILLS IN ORDER OF IMPORTANCE

1. INTERNET CONNECTION
2. CABLE
3. RENT
4. ELECTRICITY
5. PHONE
6. CREDIT CARDS
7. INSURANCE
8. MAGAZINE SUBSCRIPTIONS
9. BLOCKBUSTER LATE FEES
10. SCHOOL LOANS

You might be surprised to find electricity to be fourth instead of first cause if electricity goes out then cable and Internet are out the window, right? That's true but after gaining a good amount of experience with dodging bills you'll find that certain services have breaking points before shutting things off. You can coast on dodging an electricity bill for a good three months before they even start seriously threatening you.

My Relationship with TV Over the Years

AGES 10 AND UNDER

My relationship with TV goes way back. Back to Saturday mornings when I'd run downstairs with a bowl of Fruity Pebbles and sit up close to the screen and watch cartoons. Those were the salad days of TV. When TV could do no wrong. Even the commercials were all for you. Toys and candy. Everything TV gave was dead-on. The shows were simple and pure. And quality. Super Friends. Bugs. Yogi. There were five channels. No confusion. No annoyances. I knew where it all was. TV and me. Best buds 4eva!

AGES 11–15

Then cable came. Old TV was gone in a flash. Some guy came and left a big box that made *click-clack* noises and sat on top of the TV. There were bizarre new channels. Channels that were just for cooking or Jesus. Lots of the channels I didn't want to watch at all. The commercials were for stuff I could never buy. I started to get jealous of people who were on the TV. MTV came and showed me what a really friggin good idea was. The idea being MTV itself. I got jealous of that idea. That I wasn't old enough to think of it first.

Cause I definitely would have thought of it first. I started flipping channels around. One hand on the box. One in a bag of chips. I adjusted to new TV but somehow it felt like a change I never asked for or wanted. TV and me were still friends though.

AGES 16–21

This is when TV completely turned on me. TV started to make me feel bad about me. I started getting concerned that I had the wrong clothes. I started to buy things that I didn't really need or things that I needed but they didn't really work. Like zit cream and stuff. It was tricking me. It made my feel my friends weren't as cool as they should be. All of a sudden I didn't feel like I was watching TV anymore. I felt like TV was watching me. TV wasn't my friend. TV judged me! Who is TV to judge me? Who does TV think he is? I had to keep my eye on TV constantly so he didn't get the drop on me.

AGES 22–PRE-NOW

This was a period of time when I felt I was smarter than TV. I learned what TV did to me before. I could see through all the little tricks about TV. The commercials weren't tricking me anymore. I didn't consciously get fooled into buying stuff. I knew why I watched the shows that I watched and saw right through them. Cartoons got supersucky and weirdly Japanese. Television wasn't sticking for me anymore. I didn't want to be like the people on TV. I wanted to be everything *but* the people on TV. I was watching it nonstop to make sure I wasn't becoming anything like TV—but TV and me were no longer friends. We were having a staring contest with each other.

NOW

Television and me have come full circle. We now have a deep understanding of each other. And TV proved itself a real pal cause now that I have nothing to do and nowhere to go TV is there for me. 24/7. And for that I realize that TV is a true friend. Whenever TV is needed, TV is there. I've adjusted to his five hundred channels and have grown to appreciate them. The cartoons improved. Television has really grown up over the years. (Although my actual TV set hasn't. My RCA from 1986 still works just fine thank you.)

When I lost my job who was there for me right off the bat trying to cheer me up? TV. And when I wanted to see a chick in a bikini, who said, "Here's *Baywatch* for ya, buddy"? And who showed me stuff that I never thought I'd see? TV did. In full color. Crisp digital. Fake real reality.

But unfortunately TV seems to have lost something along the way. So I search constantly for the sparkle of TV from back in the day. The innocence of TV is gone. It's now only a glimmer. A memory. We're still friends and all but it's like an old marriage now. Comfortable. And appreciative. We have our differences. But beneath it all . . . still completely in love.

Here Are a Few Facts I've Learned from the TV

• Spiders are arachnids not insects. Insects have six legs and three bodyparts. Spiders have eight legs and two bodyparts. Plus insects often have antennae and wings. Spiders don't. Which is good cause flying spiders with bobbily antennae would be way scary.

see?

• In Egypt there is a pyramid called the Bent Pyramid. They said on the show that it was like a prototype before they built the big giant pyramids and it was shaped weird cause the architect fucked up. Those pyramids are frickin weird in general.

• There are these fish called the "deep sea anglerfish" and they're frickin weird. They live way down in the ocean in the pitchdark. Anglerfish mate by the male attaching himself to the female anglerfish permanently. He gives her sperm and she gives him food. They eventually fuse into one being. Plus there is this weird blue light sticking off its head. There's some seriously bizarre stuff going on way down in the ocean.

WEIRDO FISH LOOKS LIKE THAT

• I learned something about "body language." They talked about how you sit, and if you blink a certain way, and movement of the hands, and all that, all send messages to the person you're talking to. Thanks to that show I'm sure my new message to people will be about how I'm totally self-conscious about my body language.

• I found out the term "computer bug" actually started when a bug got mushed in one of those big giant computers back in the day. Stupid bug. Stupid computer.

THE ORIGINAL COMPUTER BUG

- I watched a show about Oklahoma State Penitentiary and there's like a bunch of dudes on death row there. They always get executed at two past midnight for some reason. This dude John Hooker was working on his appeal. He seemed like a nice guy. Actually all the death row people seemed real nice in the interviews.
- When they unearthed the city of Pompeii they found shops, clay pots, and furniture. But they also found boners. Lots and lots of boners. Paintings of dudes with big boners, boneresque sculpture, even a big ol' clay boner in the oven to make sure the bread would "rise." The image of the boner (I mean "male phallus") was used to ward off evil spirits as well as heighten the spirits.

After getting a head full of useless stuff like that you'll forget all about Yapper. In fact he'll go back into hibernation till about 2:00 A.M. He's nocturnal for the most part. If you miss him already, don't worry. He'll be back.

Watch as Many TV Channels as Possible

I've done extensive research and found out that some people like certain TV shows that other people don't like. And vice versa. I found this to be interesting. Also women watch some shows that guys don't watch. But it's important to stay informed on what other people are watching cause you don't want to be closed-minded. So when watching TV I try to watch as many channels as possible. So I can be well aware of any global conspiracies or find out new things to get chicks.

The most important thing when attempting to watch dozens of channels in one sitting is the remote control control.

REMOTE CONTROL CONTROL

If you're like me your remote control disappears alot. And you want your remote control on or near you at all times. If it disappears you're no longer doing nothing. You're doing something. You're looking for the remote control and you're pissed off. Here's what you can do to prevent loss of the remote control:

REMOTE CONTROL CONTROL

79

Tape it to your palm. Some may think this is a little extreme but it is the best way to prevent remote control loss. Be careful though cause if you go to swat a fly you might change the channel accidentally and miss something.

Tie one of those beeper/clapper things to it. This is always a cool thing. If you attach something that beeps when you clap to the remote this will be excellent. However I don't know if those things exist. Maybe I'll start a business and sell them. I'll get started on that tomorrow. Don't steal my idea or I'll sue or something.

Buy multiple remote controls. It's always good to have a backup remote. If you lose one you can also lose valuable nothing time doing the looking thing. If you have a backup you're set. Always keep this backup in the pocket of your robe for easy access. Also keep gum in your pockets too. It's always good to have gum.

Over time you'll find your speed with the remote control gets to be expert level. You fancy it up with a flip here or there. Your thumb dexterity becomes your number one skill. You can pop open lids of Pringles cans just with your thumb. And if people come over to thumb wrestle they're in for it. Sometimes I thumb wrestle myself just to stay in training.

However, in case of emergency and you totally lose the remote:

Drag the TV over closer to the couch so you can change the channels with your toes. This is good because it improves your toe dexterity. And when someone asks you one day, "How's your toe dexterity?" you'll be able to say, "Actually pretty frickin good. Almost as good as my thumbs."

Creating Your Own Show

After sitting and watching TV alot you might notice how it totally sucks.

You might think you can do better and wanna make your own show. I think that too sometimes. Here are some ideas I had for some new shows:

SITCOM IDEA

Take the rap group Ca$h Money Millionaires and banish them to Vermont. (They want to get away from thug life or something.) Have them move into a small town and try to fit in. They should have wild parties. Their hizzouse should be all done up crazy with Jacuzzis and stuff and they drive around in Escalades with twenty-inch dubs. The Vermont people are at first scared of the Ca$h Money Millionaires but at the end of each episode the Ca$h Money Million- aires end up helping the community and they all party uncomfortably. One of the Ca$h Money Millionaires can become mayor eventually. I'd call it: *Yo! What Up V-T.*

DRAMA IDEA

Dramas need to be serious. Here's the idea for this one. Take a single mom who is a doctor. Her husband mysteriously disappeared a year or so ago. She's working in the ER and some guy comes in all messed up. He tells her some secret about the whereabouts of her husband and then dies. She sets off on a journey with her daughter to find the husband and along the way uses her doctor skills like all *MacGyver*-y. It's sort of like *The Fugitive* but with a doctor chick and a kid. And like *MacGyver*. The kid can be a good scammer.

I call it: *The Search for Douglas Baker.*

Ok maybe that ain't so great but whatever. They can't all be gems. Plus I'm frickin giving these ideas away in a book and stuff. How great can they be?

GAME SHOW IDEA

You take four people and you stick them down in the sewer and you make them live there for a year. They can only come out of the sewer between 2:00 and 4:00 A.M. to do whatever. Like rats. Other than that it's back in the sewer. It's a sewer reality show. They have to set up a home and stuff down there . . . and like fight rats? . . . ok, ok that sucks . . . I can do better than that. Hold on. By the way I call that one *Sewer City*.

Ok here's a better idea for a game show and it doesn't involve the sewer. Here's the idea. You have four contestants and one big fat guy who never says anything. He's the judge. Each of the contestants has to cook a special dish for the fat guy. Here's the catch. Each dish involves a stunt of some kind. If you're barbecuing you have to walk across hot coals. If you're cooking seafood you have to dive for it without an air tank. If it's chopping you get tied up to a board and spun around while someone throws knives at you. Make it a *Fear Factor* type of show but with food. With recipes for the folks at home. At the end the fat guy tastes all four and decides who wins. That person gets twenty-five grand. The others all get paint thrown on them and pushed down in a puddle.

I call it: *We Dare You to Cook It!*

Some Real Television Secrets

- If you call up your cable company and complain about the poor reception on your TV they'll eventually give you a free month or free pay channel or something.
- If you steal cable, never respond to a freebie offer or something like that. Sometimes those ads are only directed at people who steal cable to nail them and stuff.
- If you want to have a public access show but can't afford it there are grants available that will pay for your dopey show that no one will watch. Our tax dollars at work.

Some Television Myths

Myth 1

- If you take a large spaghetti strainer and tape a baby monitor inside and thread copperwire through the holes of the spaghetti strainer then put the whole thing up on your old TV antenna on your roof it will function as a satellite dish.

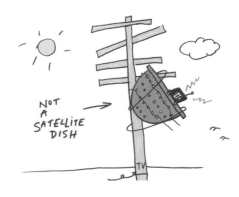

NOT A SATELLITE DISH

Untrue.

Myth 2

NOT A 30 SECOND TIME MACHINE

- If you want to get the illegal adult channels you can get them free if you send a letter with a picture of yourself shirtless to Mel Grumman, P.O. Box 204, Cleveland, OH 44070. **It's simply not true.** Mel is just a sicko with a P.O. box spreading rumors.

Myth 3

- If you put your microwave on top of your TV and a blender on top of that and a hair dryer on top of that you'll go back in time thirty seconds. **This is not true either.** It only appears that way cause sometimes it causes a minor sparkly explosion.

More Top-Secret Television Secrets

Here are some secrets about TV that alot of people might not know about:

TELEVISION DOTS

If you sit really close to the TV and stare at it from like an inch away you'll see that the TV picture is made up of little dots. If you let your eyes go lazy and just absorb the color through your eyes eventually it gives you tingles in the back of your head and you hear haikus about trees in a whispery voice.

WATCHING STATIC

If you watch static on the TV for a really long time eventually you'll see shapes. Sometimes they're faces and sometimes they're letters. Once I even saw the future but it was only five seconds into the future and the image was me watching static on the TV.

DEAD TV HOSTS

If you watch TV between 4:00 and 5:00 A.M. on UHF channel 61 it broadcasts from beyond the grave. TV talk shows continue after the host passes away. I've watched Ed Sullivan and Steve Allen. Also cause it's in another local dimension they can hear you when you say stuff. Like if you yell stuff out you can disrupt the show. If you throw stuff at the screen they get mad too and then little worker octopi travel out of the TV through the speakers and whop you on the head with foam-rubber bats. The octopi smell like Elmer's glue.

4:37 P.M.

Outside Time

Although staying inside is the best way to accomplish nothing, at times you may feel the need to go outside. There are two reasons why you might want to avoid going outside. No health insurance and no mon-ay.

When you're living on a tight budget you might have to make cutbacks on your everyday stuff. But you still have to go out for the essentials:

- Cook-ays
- Beer
- Porn
- Pringles

And:
- Porn

Plus most of the outside world involves shopping in general. Buying clothes, music, and stuff. Because you have no mon-ay this makes the outside world not easy. You might find yourself often with your face pushed up against the glass of store windows and gazing in at stuff. Or wandering around the store making lists of things you plan to buy once you have mon-ay again. Making extensive lists of random products while you're walking around may seem practical but it's not. It's a sign you might be going a bit nuts. If you find you're making lists and mumbling to yourself about how the world is too commercial it might be best for you to maybe go back inside and lay low for a bit.

You'll find that if the essentials you buy outside eat up what little mon-ay you have you might fall behind in your health insurance payments. This is a very bad idea but if it does happen make sure you take extra precautions when you're outside. One broken leg and you'll be broke for the next five years. Which would suck totally.

Here are things to avoid outside if you have no health insurance:

- Climbing rusty chain-link fences with barbed wire at the top
- Starting a fight with people who look like they're armed
- Getting yourself thrown through a plate glass window
- Getting run over by car, truck, or steamroller
- Practicing stunts
- Skiing/snowboarding/sledding
- Hurdles

- Falling off ledges
- Stuff that is poisonous
- Anything sharp
- Hitting your head on or with something big
- Large machinery
- Bricks

Also anything that ends in the letters *ER.* For example:

- Shredder
- Thresher
- Chopper
- Mower
- Tractor (whatever—it's close enough)
- Snowblower
- Acme Finger Remover

GETTiNG STiNGY STUFF iN YOuR EYE

WEiRDO BUGS

BAD BURRiTOS THAT MiGHT CAUSE DiARRHEA OR COMA

PENGUIN

FROZEN TUNDRA

JABBER JAB →

GETTiNG ALL JABBED WiTH JABBER JAB

JuMPiNG

To protect yourself outside you might want to consider wearing a helmet and also wear those glasses that you can like see behind you with and safety goggles on top of those. And knee pads. Also walk around with a whistle in your mouth in case of emergency. You may want to add a fake beard to the outfit just in case you might bump into someone and also wear tinfoil under the helmet to protect yourself from the negator-rays.

NO HEALTH iNSURANCE?
BE PREPARED!

PROTECTIVE HEAD GEAR

TiN FOiL UNDER HELMET TO DEFLECT THE NEGATOR RAYS

REARVIEW MIRROR ATTACHMENT

Goggles

WHISTLE iN CASE OF EMERGENCY

FAKE BEARD DiSGUiSE

ANTiBACTERiAL GEL

MACE →

KNEE PADS

SENSiBLE SHOES

Here Are Some Reasons for Going Outside

But I don't mean to give you too much paranoia about the outside world. If you stay inside all the time you can develop paranoias just hanging around your place. Like I once got paranoid that there was an elf jumping around my place or that some weird furry creature dressed as a superhero was hiding behind the TV. So sometimes force yourself to go outside!

FRESH AIR

You might find if you stay in your apartment for like eight to ten days straight that the air begins to get a little . . . um . . . off. It's sort of an aroma of potato chips, wet dog, and spoiled milk. This is bad. And eventually this aroma soaks into you. You might not even realize your place is stinky until someone comes over and you see his face when he walks in. His face will look like this:

If that happens it's time for you to air yourself out.

UNHERMITIZATION

You've been thinking alot about nothing in particular. And Atari. You developed a theory about how plants really rule the earth. You keep looking over your shoulder even though you're alone in your apartment. Your fingernails are long and you showered in your socks.

It's time to unhermitize. It's time to take a walk.

YOU MAY BE BECOMING A HERMIT IF....

YOU'VE BEEN THINKING ALOT ABOUT GOATS

YOU'VE GROWN SUSPICIOUS OF THE REAL INTENTION OF PLANTS

YOU START TO THINK REGULAR BUGS ARE REALLY GOVERNMENT BUGS

YOUR TOENAILS HAVE GOTTEN AWAY FROM YOU

YOU USE A GLASS TO LISTEN THROUGH THE WALL

WHAT?

YOU SAY 'WHAT?' AT NOTHING ALOT

THE NEED TO BE AROUND PEOPLE

Being around people is usually overrated but sitting around in your apartment all day like a freak may make you long for some company. But sometimes you find people can get on your nerves fast.

Be selective when you associate with people in the outside world. Any interaction that will lead to boobs in your face overrides everything of course.

ANNOYING PEOPLE OUT THERE

SPILLY SPILLERS

SHOULDER BUMPERS

FLAT-TIRE GIVERS

GOOD LOOKING PEOPLE

NON-BLINKERS

CELL PHONE SHITHEADS

STROLLING INTO A BAR

Although stopping in for a beer might seem like a good reason for going outside—it's really not that great of an idea. First reason is bars cost mon-ay and if you're going to go to a bar you should save it for nighttime. During the day there is a different type of crowd and you might end up spending hours and too much mon-ay debating things like reality shows, the new *Star Wars* movies, and conspiracy theories about the pharmaceutical industry that you'll probably make up right there on the spot and defend completely when challenged just for the hell of it. You'll also make up facts and stuff just to prove your point. This might lead to a fight, which gets us back to the health insurance situation. Plus you won't find alot of chicks in a bar midafternoon. You just don't want to start the afternoon-bar habit.

LOOK FOR STUFF

You might go out on the street to look for stuff. You'll find that more and more stuff on the curb seems like it will work for the decor of your apartment. Here are some things I've found on the street that I've brought inside:

SOME THINGS I FOUND ON THE STREET

HAM RADIO (MAYBE)?
I THOUGHT IT WAS
A HAM RADIO BUT
I PLUGGED IT IN
AND ALL IT SEEMS TO
DO IS MAKE A CLICK-CLICK
NOISE AND THEN IT STARTS
SMOKING.

UGLY LAMP
IT DOESN'T WORK BUT
IT'S A GREAT THING TO
HAVE AROUND IF YOU
EVER GET UPSET AND
WANNA SMASH
SOMETHING.

TEN-DOLLAR BILL
I WAS PSYCHED!
I SPENT IT ON
BIG LEAGUE CHEW
AND DR PEPPER.

A COPPER WIRE

SOMEONE TOLD ME
COPPER WIRE WAS WORTH
MONEY BUT NOT SURE HOW.
IT SITS IN MY HALLWAY.

Places You Can Go for Free
When You're Outside and Stuff

VISIT WORKING-FOLK FRIENDS

You might get it in your head to visit people while they're at work. Seeing people "at work" is a strange and sometimes terrifying experience. It's like stepping into a foreign country where they speak a different language. Letters will float around. FYI! CC ME! ASAP! TGIF! What do they mean? What are all these people doing? It's so noisy. They seem to be writing and typing and talking into the phone. Where is the TV? They are all fully dressed. Why? The lights may hurt your eyes. It all might get to be a bit overwhelming. If you get overwhelmed just relax and ask whoever you're visiting for a soda. Ask if there is a place you can lie down. Ask if you can have that stapler. Point at people and things. Also, you might find that the people you're visiting try to trap you. They'll ask, "You want to like send me your résumé or something? There might be a job opening here. Maybe I can hook you up with something." At this point you know you have to leave immediately or run the risk of being trapped. Stand up and nod your head. Back away slowly and lie to them about how you'll send the résumé. Smile. Put the stapler in your pocket. Look left and right. And up. Chug the soda and then bolt!

HEY!
WHATCHA
DOIN?

STOP IN AND VISIT
FRIENDS AT WORK

SHOW UP AT SOME RANDOM OFFICE

Sometimes it might be nice to show up at some random office and just sit down at some empty desk and start making phone calls. If anyone asks what you're doing there just say that John told you to work here for the day.

There's bound to be a John in that office. Then just start making phone calls. It's a good way to catch up on long-distance calls and stuff. Also it's a good reminder as to why you aren't into working cause after you make your phone calls to your friends you'll find you don't have anything to do. Just like real work. By the way if after you tell someone that you work for John and they say, "Who's John?" shoot them a look and get defensive and say, "Who are you again?" After they tell you, write down their name and put it in your pocket. When they ask why you just wrote down their name tell them it's for John's List. When they ask you what John's List is shake your head and tell them how they're obviously way out of the loop. Then turn your back on them and make another phone call.

"JOHN'S LIST" ALWAYS COMES IN HANDY WHEN YOU GOTTA SHOO SOMEONE

HANG OUT IN THE PARK

This is not a bad thing to do. You kind of walk around. Sit down and look at stuff. Yknow look at that thing over there then go over to the pond. Maybe you'll see a frog or whatever. Frogs are funny. Balloons in trees. Flowers. Put a flower behind your ear. Then you can just lie down on the grass and stuff.

THIS IS A FROG. YOU MIGHT SEE ONE IN THE PARK DEPENDING IF THERE ARE FROGS IN YOUR PARK OR NOT. IF THERE ARE NO FROGS IN YOUR PARK BUT YOU HAD YOUR HEART SET ON SEEING A FROG IN THE PARK, JUST RIP OUT THIS PAGE WITH THE PICTURE OF THE FROG ON IT AND GO TO THE PARK AND LOOK AT IT THERE.

GO TO THE BEACH

Some people like the beach. The beach is kind of free if you're near a beach. I don't like the beach for a bunch of reasons. But the main reasons are:

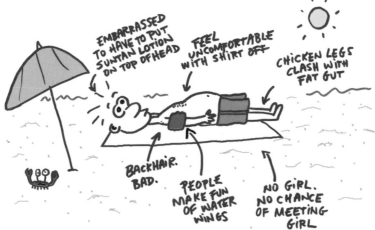

EMBARRASSED TO HAVE TO PUT SUNTAN LOTION ON TOP OF HEAD

FEEL UNCOMFORTABLE WITH SHIRT OFF

CHICKEN LEGS CLASH WITH FAT GUT

BACKHAIR. BAD.

PEOPLE MAKE FUN OF WATER WINGS

NO GIRL. NO CHANCE OF MEETING GIRL

VISIT BOOKSTORES AND LIBRARIES

Bookstores are great cause you can just sit there all day if you need to get out or whatever. The problem is that you're surrounded by books and books are boring. Except for this book! So if you're reading this in a bookstore you're psyched! Now go buy it ya mooch!

ATTEND MATIN-AY MOV-AYS

One major perk of having your days free is you can always skip out and grab a matin-ay mov-ay. Save some mon-ay! Then you can just hang out there all day and go from mov-ay to mov-ay all afternoon. You can see a month's worth of mov-ays in a single day. I once saw five mov-ays in a row. And if you want you can sit through them twice. If you don't even have the fiver or whatever just hang out by the exit door and sneak in.

Here are some things I've learned about going to the mov-ays:

Bring food. Always bring food with you. Most theaters (really *all* theaters) have a policy that you can't bring food in with you but if you go during the day the ushers don't really care. I recommend going at lunchtime and bringing a big jacket. Bagel in one pocket. Soda in the other. And buy those like chips in a can. Not Pringles . . . but like Fritos in a can or something? You know what I'm talking about? Yeah those. It's good because they don't make *crinkle-crinkle* noises.

Avoid talkers. Talking through mov-ays is probably the most annoying thing someone can do. Some people just aren't aware that there are other people in the theater. They think they're on their couch or something. So when choosing your seat sometimes you have to sacrifice the prime spots for a little peace and quiet.

If you do sit by a talker I would be careful in selecting who you confront and who you don't confront. Usually if they're dumb enough to talk in a mov-ay they're dumb enough to fight over being shushed.

Drinking at the Mov-ays. I like having a couple of beers during my mov-ays. Bring your big jacket with you and stash say two 24-ouncers. Anything bigger might be too bulky. And bring cans with you. You don't want to smash a bottle in the theater. When opening the beers just do a fake cough or sneeze to cover up the can-open noise. Nobody will bother you about drinking unless you're like sitting next to their kid or something. Who wants to confront the guy who's drinking at the mov-ay?

Top Ten Mov-ays with Unemployed People as Main Characters

10. *The Full Monty*
9. *A Clockwork Orange*
8. *Slacker*
7. *The Road Warrior*
6. *Hot Dog—The Movie*
5. *Ernest Goes to Jail*
4. *The Graduate*
3. *Cheech and Chong's Up in Smoke*
2. *The Texas Chainsaw Massacre*
1. *Office Space*

GOOD THINGS TO BRING TO THE MOV-AYS

TWO TALLBOYS
(CANS ARE BETTER THAN BOTTLES. YOU MIGHT DROP ONE.)

STRING
(FOR FIDGETING)

SMALL BULLHORN
(TO YELL 'SHUT UP!' IN THE FACE OF TALKERS)

CHIPS THAT COME IN A CAN
(NO CRINKLE CRINKLE)

MOUNDS BAR
(I LIKE MOUNDS. BRING YER OWN. WHY PAY $4.00 FOR A MOUNDS?)

ELECTRONIC QUARTERBACK
(FOR WHILE YOU WAIT. THIS GAME HAS WITHSTOOD THE TEST OF TIME.)

How to Get You Some Free Stuff and Stuff

BEG AT THE MALL

It's fun to go to the mall because you can sit and look at people and feel better about yourself. The mall is a great place to go when you want to feel good about having "voluntarily" dropped out of the rat race. You'll see people running into the Gap to buy some whatever or the dopes going into Sharper Image to get a golf club that says, KEEP YOUR HEAD DOWN . . . KEEP YOUR HEAD DOWN over and over again. Or perhaps the people who wander into the Coach store to buy a Coach wallet in the hope that when they take out their wallet someone will notice that it says Coach on it. Or how about the fools who spend a few hundred bucks on some jacket or something that's ugly and they'll be embarrassed by it a year from now when they see it in pictures?

Oh by the way, if you feel like hanging out, a mall will bum you out cause you can't buy anything . . . don't worry. Just bring a sign like this one:

Put a cup down in front of you. If you can get your hands on a Kozmo or Enron cup that would be great. People will hook you up with dollars. People are suckers for suckery stuff like that.

Here are some signs you can make to get ya some free mon-ay at the mall.

GO TO TRADE SHOWS

At trade shows they give out tons of crap and alot of times you can get in for free. Just tell the registration desk that you're a buyer. Trade show booths give out stuff like tote bags and chocolate and stuff. The problem is you might get caught up in conversation with the trade show people and you'll want out.

Here are some good ways to end the conversation if this occurs. All must be said with a straight face:

Computer trade show. "Is this compatible with my Commodore 64?"

Book publishing trade show. "You gots any of em Air-yan books? I'm sort of a Nazi wannabe."

Foodie show. (panicked) "I feel like I'm gonna puke. Oh God. I'm totally gonna puke. You got a bucket or something? It's coming up."

95

Gift show. "My gift store only sells things fifty pounds and up. I charge by the pound so that just makes sense for me. [Look at the person weirdly.] Ah, how much do you weigh? How much does your arm weigh you think? I'm interested in weight. Heavy stuff. Wait! Hold on . . . [Circle your eyes around. Pause for ten seconds.] Yeah. Weight. Fifty pounds and up."

Use any of those. Conversation over and you just earned yourself a free Frisbee or light-up pen or something.

Go Free Food Sample Hunting

Go to an ice cream store and keep asking to try flavors till they ask you to leave. Cheese shops do the same. Nice supermarkets sometimes give away samples of like dip or salami products. Once I chatted it up with the salami girl while gobbling up the samples. She was kind of cute too. Unfortunately it doesn't really work out if you want to combine hitting on people and free samples. By being all greedy with free samples you're kind of laying your cards on the table in terms of where you're at.

CRASH FORMAL OCCASIONS

It's easy to get free food and drink at any catering hall. Put on the suit or nice outfit you used to wear to work and just wander on in. As soon as you walk in the door wave to someone (no one) and give the *one-second* sign. Then wander over to the bar and get yourself a drink. Hang out by the kitchen and get yourself the appetizers as they come out first thing. Stay for a maximum of twenty minutes. That's usually the breaking point when someone will finally come over and ask who you are. Sometimes there are many formal occasions going on in one place so you can get your swerve on before getting thrown out.

HEIMLICH YOUR WAY TO A FREE MEAL

Go into a nice restaurant and order alot of food. Get a nice hunk of steak or something in your mouth. Then pretend you're choking. Push yourself away from the table and make a spectacle of yourself. Someone will come over and give you the Heimlich maneuver. Spit the meat out and continue to cough. Thank the person who "saved your life." Cry if you can.

Someone in that place will pick up your check for sure. Plus they'll all be happy that they witnessed something so amazing. In return they get a story they can tell to people for the next week. So it's kind of even steven.

4:50 P.M.

Walking Home and Checking Your Mentalness

Around this time you might start heading home. You might also find yourself talking/mumbling to yourself. It could be general conversation or simply a statement or two. This is normal but should be watched. I call these Warning Signs. Basically signs that you might be going a little mental and should check yourself:

- You come down with a case of OCD and find yourself counting your steps in multiples of fours or sixes.

- You develop superstitions or rituals around certain colors or words or animals.
- You get a twitch when you think about stuff in general.
- You realize you walked about four blocks and can't remember one thing you were just thinking about.
- You keep thinking that you recognize everyone you pass by.
- You find that the clouds are spelling words alot.
- You look down and see your clothes are on inside out or that your underwear is on the outside.
- You notice you're carrying skis.
- You feel that you're at the center of a conspiracy.
- You can't stop eating green lollipops.
- You can only look people in the eye if your head is turned away from them.
- You've decided that sunglasses are necessary all the time.

If any of those issues come up while you're walking around (yes?) just check yourself and fix your head. You'll be fine. But return home immediately.

WARNING SIGNS

HELICOPTER REINFORCES CONSPIRACY THEORY

THE SONG 'BLACK VELVET' PLAYING IN YOUR HEAD 24/7

IMAGINARY PERSON FOLLOWING YOU. WHISPERS THINGS

LOLLIPOP

YOU GOT A NEW EYE TWITCH

GOT CLOTHES ON BACKWARDS

SKI POLE

YOU COUNT TO THREE BEFORE EVERYTHING

YOU STORE STUFF IN YOUR SHOES

Back Home

Now that you're home safe, you'll find out that going outside is like tiring and stuff. You might feel a bit bad cause you were out for a while and weren't able to buy anything. This is against the American way. You may be feeling un-American cause you didn't consume.

Don't worry. Another part of the American spirit is overcoming hurdles. Making do is another part of the American way. I'll give you right here a whole bunch of coolio ideas for you to get yourself some stuff. How cool is that? Um . . . totally? It's like shopping except it's all free! And from the privacy of your own home!

How to Get Free Stuff
Without Leaving Home

Although you do have to spend mon-ay eventually on stuff there are alot of ways to get stuff for free too.

Here's some stuff you can try:

GO TO THE IMAGINARY BEACH

Since you won't be traveling much outside of a three-mile radius for a while it's sometimes good to imagine you are somewhere else. Turn the heat up in your place all the way and turn on all the lights so it's super-bright. Put a pot in the sink and turn the water on. Then lie down on the

floor. This is just like being at the beach. Except without the sand, ocean, chicks in bikinis, dudes all walking around drunk, sun, ocean noise, birds, Popsicles, kids, Frisbees, crabs, lifeguards, volleyball, suntan lotion, boats, seagulls, planes with long messages, umbrellas, and fun. Other than that it's just like being there! Plus it's free!

DOWNLOAD STUFF

If you're on the Internet pretty much everything is free. However it is illegal to take the free stuff kind of sort of. I say you shouldn't do this! It is a crime. This is how the bad people steal on the Net. They download a program. Then type in anything they want. Software, videos (yes those kind), video games, music, e-books, whatever. It's all for the taking if you can live with the guilt . . .

WRITE LETTERS

If you write letters to companies or people asking for stuff and sound crazy in your letter they'll usually hook you up with stuff. Here are some sample letters that will lead to your getting something for free.

SAMPLE LETTERS

DEAR DR. TROPICANA,
I ASSUME YOU'RE A DOCTOR EVEN IF YOU ONLY HAVE ONE OF THOSE BULLSHIT DEGREES FROM SOME SCHOOL THAT GAVE YOU A FREEBEE DEGREE IN EXCHANGE FOR A NEW DORM OR SOMETHING. NO OFFENSE. ANYWAY, I AM UNEMPLOYED AND HAVE SCURVY. WILL YOU PLEASE CURE ME BY SENDING ME COUPONS FOR FREE OJ? PLEASE HURRY DOCTOR! MY GUMS FEEL FUNNY. I'M NOT SURE IF IT'S SCURVY OR MAYBE JUST BECAUSE I ACCIDENTALLY BRUSHED MY TEETH WITH BEN-GAY ONCE WHEN I WAS FRICKIN DRUNK.
DON'T BE A DICK DOC OR I'LL EXPOSE YOU FOR THE FRAUD YOU ARE WITH YOUR BULLSHIT DEGREE.
OK?
Odd Todd

DEAR DR. SCHOLL,
MY FEET STINK SOMETHING FIERCE! WHEN I TAKE MY SOCKS OFF MY HERMIT CRABS GIVE ME A LOOK LIKE, "DUDE! UGH! DO SOMETHING ABOUT THAT STENCH!"
THIS IS WHY I AM WRITING TO YOU DR. SCHOLL. I CURRENTLY DO NOT HAVE A JOB SO I HAVE NO MON-AY FOR FOOT SPRAY. WILL YOU DONATE SOME SPRITZ TO FIX MY FEET? THEY SMELL LIKE DORITOS BUT... WRONG.
SINCERELY
STENCHILY YOURS,
+ODD
PS. MY CRABS WANT TO KNOW IF YOU CAN OVERNITE IT.

DEAR CAP'N CRUNCH,
I KNOW YOU'RE VERY BUSY THINKING UP NEW COLORS AND STUFF. DO YOU LIVE ON THAT PIRATE SHIP TO AVOID TAXES? DID YOU EVER STAB ANYONE IN THE NECK? IF YOU SEND ME A BOX OF CRUNCH BERRIES I'LL LET YOU USE THIS NEW COLOR I THOUGHT UP. IT'S CALLED ROB-BERRY. THE COLOR IS STRIPED. THINK ABOUT IT.

AYE AYE CAP'N,
Odd Todd

P.S. DID YOU EVER GET SUED BECAUSE YOUR CEREAL RIPS UP THE ROOF OF PEOPLE'S MOUTHS?

DEAR JEFF BEZOS,
I WAS GOING TO WRITE A LETTER LOADED WITH LIES ABOUT MY FAMILY. I WAS ALSO GOING TO MAKE UP SOME OUTRAGEOUS LIES ABOUT YOUR FAMILY. I WAS ALSO GOING TO WHISPER SECRETS.

ANYWAY, I BET PEOPLE ORDER STUFF FROM AMAZON AND BREAK IT THEN SEND IT BACK TO YOU AND PRETEND YOU BROKE IT FIRST. I WAS WONDERING IF YOU CAN SEND THE BROKEN STUFF. I'M UNEMPLOYED AND NEED PROJECTS.

PEACE OUT.
YOUR SECRET IS SAFE WITH ME IF YOU SEND ME STUFF.
WINK WINK.
Odd Todd

DEAR SUBWAY,
I SEEN ON THE TV THAT YOU MADE A FAT GUY MORE SKINNY.
I AM THREATENING YOU.
I WILL GAIN 300LBS IN THE NEXT 60 DAYS AND BLAME IT ON YOU. I WILL WEAR SHIRTS THAT SAY "ASK ME WHY I'M SO ROUND" AND WHEN PEOPLE ASK I WILL SAY "SUBWAY!" THIS TERRIBLENESS CAN BE AVOIDED IF YOU SEND ME LOTS OF COUPONS FOR FREE STUFF. IF I GAIN WEIGHT I'LL BLAME IT ON WENDY FROM WENDY'S.

SINCERELY,
todd

MAKE A THING OUT OF NOTHING OR SOMETHING

If you have some glue and some like weird metal things and pasta and like some wood and like broken glass and an old pair of sunglasses and some tape and you glue it all together and then tape it up it's like a sculpture. Put it on your coff-ay table. Not only did you *make* a new thing but now you *have* a new thing too! And it was free! Unless you had to go and buy glue or whatever but for the most part it was free and if push comes to shove you can get by with just tape or just like jam things together somehow or whatever. Free thing. And when you get bored with it you can sell it on eBay.

COFF-AY TABLE .
FREE SCULPTURE THING
CONVERSATION PIECE
AND BOTTLE OPENER

Also when it comes down to the holidays you can make stuff for people cause you can't buy them anything . . . cause you got no mon-ay.

Here are some presents you can make for people for their birthday or holiday or *I'm-just-glad-you're-my-friend* type of presents if you're a girl and you do that sort of thing. These are fun arts-and-craftsy things. And free!

ARTS + CRAFTSY GIFTS

SKITTLES POPSICLE STICK
PICTURE FRAME
(MAKE SURE YOU DON'T EAT
TOO MANY SKITTLES DURING
CONSTRUCTION)

MACARONI NECKLACE
(STYLISH AND
PRACTICAL)

CERAMIC ASHTRAY
WITH MYSTERY WORD

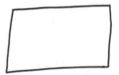

FAUX EXISTENTIALISTIC
BLANK PIECE OF PAPER
(WHEN THEY ASK YOU "WHAT IS THIS?"
JUST SAY "YOU TELL ME..."
THEN WINK)

SOCK PUPPETS
(WASH SOCKS FIRST
UNLESS PUPPET IS
'WAGS THE WET DOG')

MOLD-TERRARIUM
(JAR OF MAYO. ADD BREAD + FRUIT.
PUT IN CABINET FOR 6 MONTHS)

Around this time you'll look at the clock and say something like, "Holy crap! Is it frickin five-thirty! What the hell happened to the day?"

Just thinking about the fact that it is the end of the day might make you a little tired. Cause it will make you think about everything you've done during the day. We actually have done alot of stuff I guess and you might be thinking at this point, *What the fuck, dude? You said this was all about nothing and you got me doing all bullshit arts and crafts and shit? And writing letters and crap? WTF?* Ok ok! Jeez relax. I could have filled this book with blank pages and sealed it with shrinkwrap. Think about how pissed you'd be after the funny irony of the book itself wore off? Think about that. Now go take a powernap and get out of my hair for a while.

Late Day Powernap

THAT DREAM WILL LOOK
KIND OF LIKE THIS
(EXCEPT THE PENGUIN MIGHT BE TALLER)

During this particular nap you probably dreamed about being on all fours and under a turtle shell. You're out in the desert and there's no water anywhere. You'd like to shake off the shell cause it's really heavy but you know you need it to protect you from the sun. You crawl along and you see a penguin coming toward you. He has one of those Mexican gunfighter gun belts crisscrossing his penguin chest. He comes up to you and asks you if you've ever seen a Mexican gunfighting penguin before. You think about it and decide you haven't and ask how a penguin gets to be a gunfighter in the middle of the desert. He says, "Long story, amigo. A very long story."

If you had that dream it means you should avoid balloons. If you happen to be Canadian the penguin will more likely be a pelican.

Getting Some Cash Together

Getting back to reality you might realize that another day has gone by and you didn't make any frickin mon-ay whatsoever. Except for the dime you found while you were walking around looking at the ground and the three cents you got in the convenience store with the take-a-penny-leave-a-penny dish. Luckily, here are a few things you can do to make a quick buck:

Practice Your Act

ATTEMPTING "THE WORM"

uh! uh...

—SAD...

—DORK.

HIP HOP
BODY ROCK
DOING
THE DO
PLEASE→
GIVE

$

SYMPATHY = DOLLARS
WHEN STREET PERFORMING

If you go down on the street and leave a cup on the ground and do anything you can get some free mon-ay. It really doesn't matter what the hell you do or if you're good at it or whatever. If you just go down on the street and sing you'll make mon-ay. If you sing well people will give you mon-ay cause you're entertaining them. If you sing badly people will feel badly for you and give you sympathy mon-ay. Or if you'd like to try break dancing go for it. If you're overweight it's especially funny and people will give you mon-ay. Or get on up on a soapbox and speak out against something or say you're saving the Pink Spotted Owls or whatever. People will throw mon-ay at you out of guilt. Morally wrong? Maybe. Free mon-ay? Definite-lay.

Play the Odds

Walk down the street saying, "For five dollars I'll tell you a secret." Say it to everyone you pass by. Eventually someone will take you up on it. Usually a group of kids or something. Tell them that Coca-Cola is loaded with radon then walk away with their fiver.

Personal Community Change Jar

It's important to keep a change jar. Mine is a fishbowl. I throw all change into the fishbowl. Ask everyone who comes over to leave their change in the bowl. Tell them that it's good luck like throwing mon-ay in a fountain. Put a plastic fish in the bowl to convince the skeptics. Tell them that plastic fish are good luck in China. People will believe anything. Especially if it means there's a chance they'll get good luck at the cost of fifteen cents.

Get Some Cash Out of Some Relatives

MOM AND DAD

When you call Mom and Dad for mon-ay they usually say the same thing. "We just gave you some mon-ay! What happened to it!?" Responding to this question really depends on what your parents are like. After a while you start to get a handle on how hard you can push your parents for cash and what their breaking points are. And what they will contribute to. I don't personally know your relationship with your parents because we haven't really

hung out that much but there's two ways to go to get mon-ay out of them: threatening to move home and threatening to run off somewhere.

If your parents don't want you home threatening to move back home should always get a few bucks out of them. To reinforce the issue sleep over occasionally and act like a jerk.

If your parents wouldn't mind if you moved home then you have to threaten to run off somewhere like to some weirdo island where you can live on a dollar a day. Your parents don't need the worry of wondering if you're in some awful jail in the middle of some crazy country negotiating your way out of a good caning. They're willing to pay to have you stay put.

After you establish that relationship of give-and-take . . . well really take . . . you might have to branch out your operation to include other relatives.

SIBLINGS

Siblings are tough. You might have brothers or sisters who have extra cash lying around and you want your share. After all they're not using it. The problem with siblings is they might hold the loan over your head like a loan shark. But instead of breaking your legs they collect by making you baby-sit or take them to the airport or something. Siblings should be considered a last resort.

RICH BUSINESSMAN UNCLE

If you've got a rich uncle this could come in very handy cause you might catch him on a good day and get like five hundred dollars or something. The way you work toward this is by telling the uncle that you're looking to start your own business. Here's an idea. You're looking to start a service that will take old computers and you're going to refurbish them and sell them or donate them or something. People always wonder about old computers. Your uncle might fall for it and give you what's called *seed mon-ay*. In my experience I've found people often spend seed mon-ay on like pot seeds or something. You can spend it on whatever you want and then blame the failure of your venture on "the system."

But be careful around Uncle Businessman. He might have an opening for you somewhere in his company. If you get hooked with that just tell him you've got a cataract in your left eye but will talk to him about the opportunity after the surgery—or some lie equally outrageous.

RULE # 8½: OFTEN PEOPLE WILL BELIEVE OUTRAGEOUS LIES MORE THAN LITTLE WHITE ONES.

REALLY OLD AUNT

You might have an old aunt who has alot of cash. You might hear *ka-ching ka-ching* when you think about going to her for money. But unfortunately alot of older people lost track of inflation around 1938 and they still think fifteen dollars will set you up for the month and think they're doing you the biggest favor in the world. And you head home with your fifteen bucks after hanging out with her for a full day listening to stories about her neighbor who is always giving her mean looks and that she thinks he's involved with the *"mafia"* (whispered). But then again if you hit her up on an unlucid day you can walk away with a check for like ten grand. Usually it will be the former though.

BAD IDEAS FOR GETTING SOME MON-AY TOGETHER

JUST FYI...

SELLING ORGANS ON THE BLACK MARKET

BECOMING INVOLVED IN A SCHEME WHERE YOU'RE TRICKING THE COPS.

DELIVERING PACKAGES TO PEOPLE YOU DON'T KNOW GIVEN TO YOU BY PEOPLE YOU DON'T KNOW

HOT DOG EATING CONTESTS. THAT JAPANESE KID WILL BEAT YOU.

TAKING EXPERIMENTAL DRUGS FOR CASH. A FRIEND OF MINE DID THIS AND NOW HE CLAIMS HE HAS X-RAY VISION BUT CAN ONLY SEE THRU MATERIALS THAT HAVEN'T BEEN INVENTED YET. HE GOT $60 FOR THAT...

FREELANCE COLD CALLING SELLING THINGS OR SERVICES THAT DON'T EXIST...

Sell Stuff on eBay

If you have alot of junk lying around you'll find that some people actually want to buy your junk. You can sell it on eBay.

Here's some stuff I sold on eBay to make a few bucks:

SYNCHRONICITY ON VINYL

KOZMO MUG

VINTAGE CURE SHIRT

2MB HARDDRIVE

OLD CELL PHONE ADAPTER

BROKEN SCANNER

CHICKEN RUN DVD

APPLE II PLUS WITH TWO FLOPPY DRIVES

EGG TIMER SHAPED LIKE A DOG

Dinnertime

Here are some recipes that I like to make for dinner:

DON'T MAKE THAT

TV DINNER WITH LIGHTNING

TAKE A MICROWAVE TV DINNER AND PUT IT IN THE MICROWAVE. ADD ONE TIN FOIL BALL AND TURN ON MICROWAVE.

WARNING: I'VE BEEN ADVISED TO TELL YOU THAT YOU SHOULD NOT TRY THIS RECIPE AT HOME NOR IN SOMEONE ELSE'S HOME. SOMETHING ABOUT RADIOACTIVITY AND EXPLOSIONS. LAWYERS ALWAYS RUIN THE FUN.

BACO - BEANS

TAKE A CAN OF BEANS AND DUMP THEM IN A BOWL. THEN DUMP A LOT OF BACOS ON TOP. THEN MICROWAVE FOR A BIT.

A GOOD RECIPE IF YOU PLAN TO STAY IN FOR THE NIGHT. AS IT PRODUCES FARTS THAT HAVE BEEN DESCRIBED AS 'PUTRID' OR 'GAGGY' OR 'AWFUL' STAY HOME AND ENJOY...

PEANUT BUTTER SCOOPS

GET A JAR OF PEANUT BUTTER AND A SPOON.

SPOON GOES IN JAR. PEANUT BUTTER GOES ON SPOON. SPOON GOES IN MOUTH. SPOON GOES IN JAR. PEANUT BUTTER GOES ON SPOON. SPOON GOES IN MOUTH. DO NOT DO THIS RECIPE IF YOU ARE ALLERGIC TO PEANUTS...OR BUTTER...OR SPOONS. SNEEZING CAN BE DISASTROUS.

Think About Boobs

BOOBS!!

BOOBS!!

(If yer not into boobs in the face just skip this chapter. Also if your sense of humor has gone beyond say ninth grade then you might wanna skip it too.)

On the first draft of this book I wrote "Think about boobs!" like every third or fourth minute. My editor guy told me he thought that was kind of overkill. I told him it was reality. He said, "I'm not going to print a book that says 'Think about boobs' every frickin third line." I kind of wanted the book to come out so I decided to put the boob stuff here. Eight o'clock is primetime for boobs so it works out anyway: 8:00 P.M. Must see boob-bee! (Ok. I know there were alot of dumb jokes in this book but that one totally sucked. See what happens when you get boobs on your mind? Everything goes downhill as the thing downhill goes uphill . . . if you catch my meaning. Wink wink. See, another bad joke! Ugh! Ok let's get to the boobs.)

Fun

Boobs in the face are fun. Size doesn't matter. Big boobs. Small boobs. Whichever. Whatever. Whenever. Fun. Funny and fun!

There's Two

Boobs never get boring cause as soon as there is a glimmer of boredom with a boob there's a whole other boob! Then when you start thinking about other stuff you remember something. Another boob. There's two! And that space in between is nice.

Distraction

Boobs in the face block out all other thought and vision. Boobs make Yapper simply go out and take a walk around the block a couple of dozen times. You can't see anything but boobs. No credit card bills. No leaky faucets. No weird mole on your shoulder that you can't even get checked out cause you have no health insurance. No nothing. Nothing but boobs. Hee hee. Boobs.

So much of your day is sometimes filled with things you don't want in your face in your face. Like you might have your landlord in your face asking you where your rent is. Or you can have TV in your face pouring radiation and bad jokes all over you for hours on end. Or perhaps if you work or something your boss gets in your face telling you how you're a big flunky and how you should be "concerned." She might give you a little sit-down. To explain to you why you're not performing up to speed. She might tell you that you check your personal e-mail account too much or "seem to spend alot of time on the phone." She might accuse you of not having a full grasp of the company mission and tell you you're "not a team player." Then she might put you on some kind of "probationary period" where you have like two months to get "your act together." So when it comes down to it with all that kind of stuff out there in your face: Boobs rule. If your boss has nice boobs this can cause problems. It's a whole yin–yang thing.

RULE #9: BOOBS ARE NICE AND SOFT. AND GOOD. AND FUN. AND GREAT.

But to get to boobs in the face there's something you need to do first.

8:23 P.M.
Go Outside Again

After sitting around for a while you might feel the need to go out at night. To get booze. To maybe try and find someone who is willing to feel you up and lick your neck. And squeeze your butt. Maybe you just feel electric at night and get all up-up for outside. Whatever you want. There's a place most people go to when they think about having some stranger grope em.

Going to a Bar

Ok so we'll go out again. I know this is alot for one day so if you want you can say screw it and watch some tube. But if you wanna head out here's some things you should check before heading out:

Issues with Meeting People

One thing that prevents alot of people from talking to people is that they're shy and can't pull it together to start a conversation without feeling stupid. When you have no mon-ay and no job this makes things even worse. It's like you can't buy someone a drink cause you have no mon-ay—so you have to like offer like a sip or something and that's no good. Most people do not like sips of anything from strangers. Especially strangers who look like they just woke up.

GOING TO A BAR CHECKLIST

- ☐ FLY ZIPPED
- ☐ NO BOOGERS
- ☐ CLOTHES MATCH
- ☐ TEETH CHECK
- ☐ STAND UP STRAIGHT
- ☐ PRACTICE DANCE MOVES
- ☐ PRACTICE SPEAKING
- ☐ PRACTICE SMILE
- ☐ CHECK TO MAKE SURE YOU DON'T HAVE AN AROMA

Also there's something about the look I give people that somehow often gets misinterpreted. They say when you wanna pick someone up in a bar you have to like give the person a "look." A look that says that you're happening and like sexy and stuff. But I think my look somehow sends an altogether different message.

WHAT YOU THINK YOU LOOK LIKE

WHAT YOU LOOK LIKE TO OTHERS

MAKE SURE YOU PRACTICE WITH YOUR FACE BEFORE GOING OUT

Absolutely Terrible Pickup Lines. Do not use any of these:

- My crotch itches like a mofo.
- Something smells and I think it's you.
- I was drunk before I even got here.
- I have perma-lice.
- I am trying to control myself.
- This is my first day out since all that stuff happened.
- Can you tell my eye is fake? Wanna touch it?
- I don't like eating lobsters but I sure like cooking them.
- Your hair looks pretty. Can I have some?
- I'm into carving
- My tongue stings.
- My mom is gonna like you.
- What's your first and last name?
- Here's the first three digits of my phone number. If you want the rest they're in my back pocket. Go for it. [Then wink.]
- My futon almost has room for two.

If you do start chatting with someone, often questions come up that might stump you. Like, "What do you do?"

Some people say honesty is the best policy. But if you say something along the lines of, "Well today I woke up around ten-thirty, I unsuccessfully looked for a job for a minute or two, I fantasized about some things, took a powernap or two, and I ate potato chip crumbs off my chest," this most likely will not impress too many people. And if it did impress them you should be cautious. If those activities strike people as being ambitious you might want to avoid those folks as you can only imagine what the hell they did all day. But recommend them buying this book before you say your good-byes.

Here are some lines you should *not* use in response to "So what do you do?" Just FYI.

- I'm thinking about becoming an unlicensed physician.
- Can I be your roommate and sleep on the floor?
- It's classified. Please stop prying into my personal life.
- I analyze things. I'm analyzing you right now.
- I'm a freedom fighter and I live in the woods.
- I'm an inventor. I invented this stuff you smear on yourself to clear up this weird rash that I seem to give people.
- Do you know what a fluxbarrier is? No? Well then forget it. Dummy.
- I'm a CEO for a now defunct company that actually never existed.
- I write canine erotica.

CAN'T PICK UP CHICKS?
HERE'S A MAD LIB TO HELP

HEY _(ANOTHER NAME FOR GIRL)_ !
YOUR _(BODY PART)_ LOOKS REALLY
GOOD TONITE. I'D LIKE TO
BUY YOU A _(CHEAP BEER OR MALT LIQUOR)_
AND MAYBE WE CAN TALK A
WHILE. HEY! DO YOU LIKE
(ANYTHING) ? HAS ANYBODY
TOLD YOU THAT YOU LOOK LIKE
(FAMOUS PERSON) SORT OF? HEY!
I HAVE A _(ANYTHING AT YOUR PLACE)_ AT MY
PLACE. WANNA SEE IT? OH...
YOU GOTTA GO? OK... NICE
TALKING WITH YOU _(RANDOM GIRL NAME)_ !

Here Are Some Suggestions to Improve Your Chances of Meeting Someone and Getting Groped

- Try to get to know the bartender. I think it's always cool when someone knows the bartender and the bartender knows who they are. I have never been successful at this as I am terrible with names and don't leave an impression that lasts for more than the time it takes the bartender to get me the drink. But if you're the friendly sort know the bartender.
- Know what you want to order. Nothing more annoying than someone who responds to "What do you want?" by staring at the bottles and going, "Umm . . ." People like people who know what they want and go after it. It shows confidence and conviction. At least that's what I heard. I'm not really sure though. You better check with someone else.
- Don't think it's cool to be good at the video game in the bar. It's not. Even if you get the high score in that golf game with the big trackball. No one cares. Sorry. Also no one thinks it's funny when you put in DIK as your initials.

YOU MEAN I JUST SPENT $11.00 to GET MY INITIALS UP THERE... AND NOW YOU TELL ME IT'S NOT COOL? AT ALL?

PRO GOLF '99

50 CENTS PER GAME

- If you're a guy don't dance by yourself. Some guys might think that dancing by themselves shows how they're a free spirit and gives them an opportunity to show off their moves. I've learned that dancing by yourself is um . . . not good. If you're a girl dance all you want. Guys like me who talk to no one have to look at something besides the golf game with the trackball.

CHICKS DON'T DIG THE THROW-UP GUY

PUKE

- Don't get so drunk that you vomit on yourself or on others. I've found that having vomit on you greatly decreases your chances of hooking up. And if you vomit on someone else it decreases your chances of hooking up with that person dramatically.

Basically I don't have any other ideas on where you can meet someone if you're shy like me. Some people say libraries or supermarkets. But people like me just can't open up a conversation with someone cold like that. Maybe if you take a class or something you could meet someone there. But that brings us back to the whole no mon-ay situation.

9:30 P.M.

Walking Home All Down on Yourself

The walk home from a bar by yourself is like the real walk of shame. Seeing happy couples all strolling by arm in arm while you're on your own may make you feel a little down on yourself. There's a few things that might cheer you up:

Strip Clubs

Going to a strip bar might seem like a good idea. But strip bars are expensive and they trick you.

When you go to a strip bar you quickly get sucked into the fantasy of actually being attractive and sexy, and this goes hand in hand with alcohol

SCORES
GENTLEMEN'S CLUB

NO MON-AY?
NO BOOB-AY...
SO GO AW-AY...
AY?
BEFORE I PUNCH
YOU IN THE HEAD...
AY...

until you run out of mon-ay. Then they stamp an *L* on your forehead and you have to leave.

Diners

You might also think about stopping in a diner or something and getting some comfort food. This isn't a bad idea. Recently I went into a diner and they had something called a Rebel Burger. This was a cheeseburger with onion and bacon and mushrooms and a fried egg on top. The Rebel Burger stopped my heart for like thirty minutes. Because I had no life insurance I had to jam my finger into a lightsocket just to get things moving again. If I were you I'd avoid Rebel Burgers and anything that may make you wanna jam your finger in a lightsocket. Forget the diner.

REBEL
↙ BURGER

Go Near Water

Sometimes going near water makes me feel better. So if you're by a lake, river, or ocean just go to the water. Something about the noise. But if you can't get near water do not think a street corner puddle will do. Sitting by a street corner puddle will not make you feel better. Especially if someone drives by and splashes it all over you.

WATER
↓

Convenience Store

It's time to hit the convenience store and load up on supplies. This makes me feel better sometimes. So load up and head on home for a night of fun and excitement.

> HERE ARE SOME CONVENIENCE STORE SNACKS I LIKE

PRINGLES
(ORIGINAL ONLY)

YODELS
(SERIOUSLY UNDERRATED)

HOT FRIES
(GOOD WITH BEER)

BEEF JERKY
(HAS BUILT-IN ENTERTAINMENT BY PRODUCING GIANT BURPS)

DR PEPPER
(F-COKE)

SNO-BALLS
(DISGUSTINGLY IRRESISTIBLE)

FUDGE STRIPE COOK-AYS
(ALSO GOOD FOR BREAKFAST)

TWIX
(I LIKE TWIX)

CHIPWICH
(SPIT IN YOUR DIET'S FACE)

10:03 P.M.

Now that you struck out at the bar and have no boobs in your face and are sitting in your place with a bag full of junk food . . . you might try one last resort to meet someone. There are still people out there to meet. And you don't even have to check yourself in the mirror first.

Go Online to Find a Date

I've heard there's been alot of success dating online. I've heard rumors that people even get or put boobs in the face from online dating. But if you have no job or no mon-ay there is a problem with dating online. The problem is that form you have to fill out. It asks you all sorts of questions that are difficult for your current situation. Questions like:

- Occupation?
- Interests?
- Body type?
- Hobbies?

And:
- Ideal relationship?

PHOTO FROM SIX YEARS AGO. Looking GOOD

RECENT PHOTO TAKEN WHILE HOLDING CAMERA AT ARM'S LENGTH. BEST SHOT OUT OF THE 24 TAKEN.

Then you have to pick out a photo of yourself. This is difficult too because the older the photos are the better you look. And for me it was a substantial dropoff.

When you like to stay inside all day and watch TV. Have a beer gut. Are balding. Have smelly feet. Last thing you read was the back of a cereal box. With a fear of intimacy combined with being a freak combined with not having a job and being a goofball and the fact that you can't cook and are shy around people and are a slob. On top of that the only thing you have expertise with is video games on top of that having a hairy back and no mon-ay whatsoever . . . umm . . . makes you a tough sell.

But if you do ever find a date online there's a few places that are good to go to that don't cost alot of mon-ay or whatever.

COFF-AY

Coff-ay is a great date type thing cause it's cheap and coff-ay is good. If you go to a coff-ay shop and are waiting for your date, write in a notebook while you're waiting. When your date shows up you'll seem more interesting because you're writing. Here's a couple things I wrote while waiting for a date once:

COFF-AY SHOP

— SO YOU LIKE COFF-AY . . . AND TV . . . AND COFF-AY . . . ANYTHING ELSE?

Coff-ay Shop Writings

Jason (from Friday the 13th) Speaks Out Against Living Underwater

It ain't easy living on the bottom of a lake. It kinda bites it. First off, you can barely see anything—all the miggidy-muck swirling around all the time kinda annoys me. You gotta squint just to see your hand in front of your own face. Also I'm all bloated and googily-eyed. I thought it would be cool to live underwater and play like Aquaman games—but trust me the fun doesn't last. Plus the water makes my skin real clammy-like and it like peels off in layers that hang all around me. The ground is also kinda mushy and I'm not crazy about fish—incidentally, they don't seem to be too crazy about me either. I don't mean to complain or anything but living in that whole in-between-worlds thing is no prize. That's why alot of people go the straight-up route after croaking. But if you were a little kid and you drowned in a lake and had a choice to play Aquaman games and hang out for a while in the lake, wouldn't you be tempted? Whatever. I'm kind of evil now cause of the whole experience. All I really look forward to is the stray boat that floats overhead. Usually it carries some kinda trauma victim who just had to get away from all the murder and stuff. So I swim on up and jump out of the water, loop my arm around the neck, and drag em under. I don't kill em dead or anything—but I just like the overall effect. Once I get em under I stare at them right in the face and they are like so wowed-out once they get a good look at me. It's shocking enough just to be held underwater—but to be held by some kinda gross lake-boy is an extra kicker. But those moments are too few and far between. So anyway, if you ever get drowned in a lake and you have a choice to stay in the lake or go on to another world, I have some advice for you . . . take door number two. Living undead at the bottom of a lake rots.

The end.

MY EYE HOBBY

I GOT AN EYE
I TOOK it FROM A GUY
RIGHT OUT OF HiS HEAD
I THINK it MADE HiM DEAD
NOW I WANT ANOTHER
MAYBE FROM HiS BROTHER
ONE iN BROWN OR BLUE
I DON'T CARE FROM WHO
I LiKE THE EYEBALL FUN
 GRAB THE EYE AND RUN
OUT LOOSE ON THE STREET
STRUTTiN TO THE EYEBALL BEAT
RiP it OUT THE SOCKET
AND PUT iT iN YOUR POCKET
THiS FEELiNG NEVER PASSES
SO ALWAYS WEAR YOUR
 SAFETY GLASSES

120

Actually it might not be great to show your date what you're writing if you write poems or stories like that. Just pretend you're shy about your work or whatever. Or say it's poetry and you're insecure.

WALK IN THE PARK

Romantic and free. However, this type of activity puts an emphasis on conversation. This could be a problem if you can't think of stuff to say alot. I'm shy and sometimes not doing an activity that involves a distraction isn't great. If you do go to a park bring a Frisbee or something so you can separate and impress your date with your Frisbee stylings. If you can't throw a Frisbee though you should practice first. I practice in my apartment alot. Wrap your breakables like lamps and stuff in bubblewrap before practicing indoor Frisbee.

GO TO THE ANIMAL SHELTER

A trip to the animal shelter to adopt a pet is a good cheap date. This is good especially for guys cause it makes you look sensitive. You can go as far as to adopt a pet to score points and then just return it like a day or two later. If you continue dating and your date asks, "What happened to the cat?" just say the cat was a lemon—and you had to return it.

LEMON CAT

DEF. CAT POOPS ON FLOOR
CAT FARTS ALOT
CAT MEOWS NON STOP.
CAT GOES CRAZY WHEN PICKED UP
CAT RUINS STUFF
CAT THROWS UP ON PILLOW
CAT HATES YOU
CAT PLOTS AGAINST YOU
CAT THINKS IT'S SMART.

OTB

Many people think going to the OTB is a good place for a first date. The OTB is bad for alot of reasons. Mainly cause you have no mon-ay to be gambling right now and without betting on stuff the OTB can get extremely boring. And you'll find the horses that win are always the horses you would have picked and this could get frustrating. Plus if you're a guy your date might be the only chick in the place and might feel uncomfortable because guys will ask her to kiss tickets for good luck and stuff. Anyplace that makes a chick feel uncomfortable or threatened is probably bad for a first date.

And stay away from restaurants in general . . . unless it's cafeteria style.

10:39 P.M.

Snacky Snacks at Home

Ok enough of the dating crap. Whatever with that. It's time for some late-night snacking!

If you changed out of your robe to go out, immediately change back into it. Sit down on the couch and spread your convenience store booty in front of you. Your snacks should be eaten in the following order:

1. Appetizer: Sno Balls
2. Salad: Andy Capp's Hot Fries
3. Main course: Beef jerky with a side of Funyuns
4. Dessert: Twix
5. Après dessert: Chipwiches

If you want you can swap the Twix and Sno Balls. It depends on your personal taste. And enjoy yourself. Don't worry about your gut. No one is looking and at the very least while times are tough . . . at the very least you can have a few Sno Balls and Chipwiches.

11:03 P.M.

Watch the News

It's good to stay informed about the news for alot of reasons. The main reason is to find out if there is an escaped lunatic in your neighborhood. Once you get the sign-off on that, you can settle in to the news. They'll probably talk alot about the economy and if you're lucky they'll parade a greedy scumbag in handcuffs for us all to see and throw mental eggs at. And then they'll talk about how the world is all messed up and stuff. This will make you feel better about being personally messed up. And your place in the world will be clear as we're all in this together and each one of us, in our own special way, is totally messed up. So be open and honest with your messedupness. The scariest people out there are the ones who hide their messedupness or are convinced that they're not messed up at all. These are the people to stay away from cause they have weird habits at home and they might put you on some kind of list they have or something.

Be free! We're all a little screwed up! Be proud!

11:35 P.M.

Ending Procrastination

It's around 11:35 that you might have realized that you haven't done any "real-life" things and feel like you need to get this stuff together before you get ready for bedtime. The best thing to do is make a list of the things you need to do. This might include:

LATE NITE TO DO LIST

- ☐ GET BILLS TOGETHER
- ☐ BUY WEDDING GIFT FOR WEDDING 362 DAYS AGO
- ☐ DO DISHES
- ☐ GET LAUNDRY TOGETHER
- ☐ ATTACK SOAP SCUM
- ☐ CUT TOENAILS
- ☐ SHAVE
- ☐ HARASS MCI AGAIN
- ☐ "BE" WITH SELF
- ☐ CHANGE THOSE FRIGGIN SHEETS!

Once you put this list together it will make you realize that you can't possibly do the things you need to do this late at night. Much better that you should put this off till tomorrow. Plus you'll feel a little better cause you actually put the list together in the first place.

Now on to other things you can do:

Late-Night Thoughts

It's quiet late at night. It's time to unwind. You might watch a little TV. You might just relax and play a video game. Write some e-mail. IM with someone. Perhaps call a friend who's up late at night.

This is your time. Your time to let your body and mind relax and do the things you need to do to go to sleepyland.

Brush your teeth.

Wash your face.

Take notice of the moon.

You've had a very full day and can relax with a sense of accomplishment. You've done quite a bit and need this time to process it all.

So you might not have found a job today. That's ok.

So you may not have found a date today. That's ok too.

So you didn't make any mon-ay today. So what?

So you ate junk food and watched tons of TV. You're American.

So you may be an outcast of society now. Great. Join the club.

So you may be grasping at threads to maintain a respectable place in the world. Respect is overrated.

125

You are good. You are talented. You have something to offer this world. You can find it. Tomorrow really try to focus on bringing yourself one step closer to your dream. Someone has to do what you want to do. Why shouldn't that person be you?

Have confidence in yourself and what you want to get out of life. Go for it! You have the time now to do something with your time. Strive for it. Push yourself and go after what will make you most happy.

Climb into bed with the self-assurance that you *can* do it. And tomorrow you will . . .

RULE #10: YOU CAN DO IT.

1:00 A.M. – 4:00 A.M.

It's around this time that Yapper will come to tuck you in. Yapper will snuggle up next to you and sing a lullaby to you. Well maybe not a lullaby exactly. More like whispering in your ear everything there is to worry about . . .

It's tomorrow. Turn to page 1.

About the author

Todd Rosenberg currently lives in Brooklyn. His landlord won't let him get a dog so he lives with two hermit crabs. He can be reached at oddtodd7@hotmail.com